FAMILIAR STRANGERS

MARLENE SWAY

Familiar Strangers

Gypsy Life in America

8 January 2001

To Carol —

I hope this book makes you an enthusiastic student of Gypsy life.

With best wishes,

Marlene Sway

University of Illinois Press   URBANA AND CHICAGO

© 1988 by the Board of Trustees of the University of Illinois
Manufactured in the United States of America
C 5 4 3

This book is printed on acid-free paper.

Library of Congress Cataloging-in-Publication Data

Sway, Marlene, 1950—
    Familiar strangers : gypsy life in America / Marlene Sway.
        p.   cm.
    Bibliography: p.
    Includes index.
    ISBN 0-252-01512-6 (alk. paper)
    1. Gypsies—United States—Social life and customs.   I. Title.
DX201.S98 1988   87-20449
973'.0491497—dc 19   CIP

To my parents Shirley and Eugene Sway,
  my husband Dean Ramus,
  and to Little George,
  a Kalderash Gypsy boy,
  as an affirmative answer
  to his question,
  "We're human, ain't we?"

CONTENTS

ACKNOWLEDGMENTS

I owe the greatest debt to my Gypsy informants who took the risk, to varying degrees, to trust a non-Gypsy with information about their society. There are a number of Gypsies who stand out in my mind to whom I am especially grateful, but because they prefer to remain anonymous I cannot explicitly name them here. They know who they are.

Among those Gypsies to whom I am most thankful are three California *Rom Baro*, or chiefs. Without their willingness to help me I would have never collected such rich data. I thank them for answering my questions and for inviting me to weddings, *slavas*, and *pomanas* over the years. I am particularly grateful to one *Rom Baro* for telling me his true Gypsy name and then providing me with telephone numbers and connections to Gypsy chiefs living in Utah and Alabama.

I will always be thankful to and hold dear Little George, an adolescent Kalderash boy. Little George met with me regularly during the writing of this study. Typically we met at my father's store, Sway and Sway Company, and then went to a variety of local spots to work. George served me admirably as an informant, teacher, and friend. Little George attempted to teach me Romany, the Gypsy language. Not only was Little George a patient teacher, but he was also a teacher who took his job seriously and often prepared lessons for me before we met. I still have and will always cherish the lessons he prepared for me, sometimes on the reverse side of cardboard boxes. My Romany lessons include those for numbers, money and valuables, family members, animals, fruit, vegetables, household items, the fortunetelling business, the body and fender business, and religious beliefs and practices. Having completed the fifth grade, Little George understood the way in which non-Gypsies learn. He pointed out the long and short vowel sounds when trying to teach me how to pronounce a Romany word, and he always became frustrated when I had trouble with the Gypsy "r" sound, saying "if you grew up speaking Spanish instead of English, you wouldn't have trouble with the r's." Little George also served as a truth checker on information I had obtained from other Gypsies. He was a sophisticated clearinghouse of information. When I suspected that other Gypsies had given me erroneous information or conflicting messages, Little George would always correct it. He took pains to explain the Gypsy logic behind disinformation, and then he set the record straight; he was a stickler for detail and accuracy. I owe him so much.

There were many non-Gypsies who supplied me with information about Gypsies they knew through some professional relationship. I am indebted to three California welfare workers who specialize in Gypsy cases. Because these people will go on working with Gypsies, it is not fair for me or any other researcher to reveal their names. As with my Gypsy informants I will use pseudonyms when referring to them. There were also many city attorneys, physicians, nurses, and public school teachers who served as informants in this study. I want to thank them all.

In the academic realm, there are several people at UCLA who merit my praise and appreciation. First, I thank Ivan Light for his constant guidance and encouragement during the writing of this book. It was Dr. Light who insisted that I look at economic behavior as a key to the Gypsies' survival as an ethnic group; he was right about this and many other points of investigation. I am happy to have him as my mentor. Second, I want to thank Kenneth Bailey and Edna Bonacich (UC-Riverside) for their influence and suggestions in the writing of this study. I also want to thank Barisa Krekić and Georges Sabagh who served on my dissertation committee and contributed helpful advice and support.

Beyond the academic world of UCLA is my dear friend Rocky, who unselfishly devoted countless hours advising me on this book. Rocky has been my guiding light. I will always be grateful to him for his help on this book and for his genuine friendship.

Along the way there were many nonacademic people who assisted me simply out of goodness and maybe a slight fascination with Gypsies. My research in Richmond and Williamsburg, Virginia, in 1980 could not have been sustained without the help of Julia and Frances Neal. They provided me with shelter, food, and transportation when necessary, making my research possible on a minimal budget. I am very thankful to them for their kindness and generosity.

On a personal level, I want to thank my devoted husband, Dean

Ramus, for his love and belief in me. Dean would never let me give up and has made countless sacrifices so this book and my career could continue. Although not trained as a sociologist, Dean has become my valuable ally in research. He has a keen eye for observation and has provided me with wonderful insights throughout the data collection and writing of this book. I was lucky to find a husband who is so fair, funny, and concerned about humanity.

In acknowledging my parents, I want to thank my loving and inspirational mother, Shirley Sway, for all her help and support over the years. I will always be grateful to her for instilling in me the notion that I should find work with a purpose. I want to thank my father, Eugene Sway, for caring about people over profit and making Sway and Sway Company a place where all people felt comfortable. If he had not created such a friendly atmosphere, the Gypsies would never have returned year after year. Without Sway and Sway Company I could have never cultivated the trust of many of my Gypsy informants, and this book could have never been written.

Behind every book is a group of people who are instrumental in a number of ways. From the bottom of my heart, I want to thank my editor at the University of Illinois Press, Lawrence J. Malley, for his dedication to this project and constant good cheer. Larry has made sure that every phase in the production of this book has gone smoothly, and it has been a sincere pleasure working with him.

I want to thank my former departmental chairman Hobson Bryan for allocating departmental resources in the typing of this manuscript. I will always be grateful to Sandra Lavender for the excellent job she did in typing this manuscript and all the correspondence associated with its publication. Sandra's dedication to the task and her even disposition made the entire process easier. Thanks should also go to Linda Crowson for assisting in a million small ways to ensure that necessities were accomplished. I want to express my gratitude to Irving Leftoff, my uncle, for giving me his IBM Selectric so I could type the original version of this study.

Lastly, I want to thank Sage Publications for their permission to use revised sections of two articles which appeared in *Urban Life:* "Economic Adaptability: The Case of the Gypsies," 13(1984):83–98; and "Traveller-Gypsies," 14(1985):236–39. Additionally, I want to thank Marilyn Affleck, editor of *Free Inquiry in Creative Sociology,* for granting me permission to use revised parts of my article "Fortune Telling Practice Among American Gypsies," 15(1987):3–6.

Chapter 1

INTRODUCTION

𝓶 Y FASCINATION with Gypsies began in childhood. At age seven I remember encountering Gypsies regularly in my family's army surplus store in Los Angeles. For the last thirty-five years, this store, Sway and Sway Company, has been a magnet for Gypsy shoppers. Although I never analyzed why we had a steady stream of Gypsy customers, I looked forward to meeting and talking to them in the store. Now I realize that Gypsies were attracted to Sway and Sway Company because my father, willing to conduct business on their terms, never discriminated against them. The Gypsy customers could always talk my father into paying the sales tax for them, and he would haggle over prices until a satisfactory outcome was achieved for everyone.

Beyond the financial aspects, my father showed a sincere respect and interest in Gypsy life. He spoke to them as normal citizens, not suspicious characters, and over time he developed a number of friendships with his Gypsy customers. The Gypsies visited our family business not just to buy something and leave; instead they stayed for hours, talking to my family and meeting other Gypsies. By word of mouth, Gypsies far beyond Los Angeles heard about my father's store and shopped there when they were in town.

Down the street from Sway and Sway Company was a funeral parlor that did business with Gypsies. Since Gypsy funerals often last three days, it was common to find Gypsies camping in the funeral parlor's parking lot. Hundreds of Gypsies would attend these funerals, often staying the full three days or longer. During these times they also shopped at Sway and Sway Company. I still do not know if the Gypsies found our store because of the funeral parlor or if they found the funeral parlor because of our store. In any event, the block around my father's store was always a hub of Gypsy activity.

Over the years my family's relationships with Gypsy customers grew more involved and deeper than just patron-customer relationships: we were invited to weddings and summer barbeques; we learned of the Gypsies' family and health problems; we heard about business opportunities that soured. And because the majority of the Gypsies we knew were illiterate, we read letters, report cards, prescription instructions, and appliance warranties for them.

My Relationships with the Gypsies

When I was fourteen, I attended the wedding of a Gypsy girl I had known since I was seven years old. Every detail of the wedding intrigued me because I identified so closely with the bride—she was my age. I sensed the girl was both excited and scared. She was excited because her father had received a good bride price for her and overnight she would be transformed into a woman capable of handling the responsibilities of married life. She was scared because she was going to leave the sheltered existence of her Los Angeles family and live in Chicago with the groom's family. After the wedding I saw the girl's family regularly. A year and a half later, the girl returned home to her family; divorce proceedings began, and she was very depressed. Because the boy's family had overworked her and he had beaten her, the *kris*, the Gypsy tribunal, determined that her family be allowed to keep all of the bride price as compensation for her mistreatment and loss of virginity. From this marriage I gained tremendous insight into Gypsy culture: how marriages were arranged, how bride prices were determined, how adolescents became adults overnight, and how the Gypsy community handled life's mistakes. During that time I became a committed but informal student of Gypsy life.

From the time of that wedding until I graduated from college, I worked in my family's store every Saturday and during school vacations; thus, I had weekly contact with many Gypsy families. I used slack periods at the store to get to know the Gypsies better. For a couple of years I arranged to teach two Gypsy brothers how to read. Every Saturday, unless they were out of town with their families, the boys appeared with their school readers. When they first started school they were behind the other students, but after six or seven months of tutoring they were able to read better than most students in their grades. After two years the brothers moved to Texas with their family. Years later they came to the store especially to introduce me to their new brides. The brothers had married two sisters through a double arranged marriage in Texas. They said they stopped to pay their respects to me since I was the one who taught them how to read as children.

Other Saturdays were spent with young Gypsy women who asked me endless questions about the foreign world of high school and dating; most Gypsies I have encountered stopped attending school at ten or eleven years old, and they are never permitted to date. Being equally curious about life for a Gypsy teenager I asked them questions abut their crushes, fantasies, and hopes for the future. I learned that romance was not given much credibility in the Gypsy community and that ultimately they would all become fortunetellers whether they were interested in the occupation or not.

During these Saturday conversations various Gypsy girls taught me how to tell fortunes. They explained that they really did not believe in it but had to convince the customer. The girls explained how they "read" a person before they looked at their palm; they taught me how to examine faces, hands, body language, clothes, jewelry, and any other aspect of the customer that would betray socioeconomic status, general health, and self-confidence. Although I ultimately learned to be a fairly well-trained fortuneteller, my fortunetelling training taught me much more than reading palms. The interactions surrounding the technique revealed the attractions, fears, and attitudes Gypsies held about the dominant society.

While I enjoyed the contact I had with Gypsies, I never realized that my experience was unusual; I assumed most people living in California had dealings with Gypsies. I first realized how unusual my experiences were in 1972 during an undergraduate seminar on minority groups. After I selected Gypsies as the ethnic group I wanted to research for my term project, I noticed that my professor and the other students had no knowledge of Gypsies; in fact, my classmates were startled to discover that Gypsies lived in the United States, let alone Los Angeles. The class believed that Gypsies were overwhelmingly concentrated in eastern Europe, traveling in brightly painted caravans.

My library research for this term project revealed other surprises. Very little social science research had been conducted on Gypsies in the United States; hard statistical and demographic data did not exist on American Gypsies; and they were not enumerated in the census. Instead, many of the library's holdings on Gypsies were romantic accounts written by non-Gypsies who claimed to have lived with Gypsies as children or during a rebellious phase in their adult lives. These accounts were colorful but useless in trying to prepare a careful report on Gypsies.

What did exist at UCLA's Research Library was a journal spanning almost one hundred years that devoted itself to Gypsy life and lore. *The Journal of the Gypsy Lore Society* published contributions from mostly European scholars on the history, linguistics, religious observances, lore, and folk customs of European Gypsies. Occasionally contributions in this journal dealt with Gypsies in the Americas. While the journal did not focus on social science research, the thousands of entries gave me a very broad understanding of Gypsies as a people, and numerous articles provided a rich background for comparing Gypsies in various societies during many historical periods.

In the fall of 1974 I entered graduate school to pursue a doctorate in sociology with the ambition of conducting a serious sociological study on Gypsies. The preceding summer, I had traveled to Yugoslavia with the hope of observing Gypsies in an eastern European country. Given my inability to speak Romany or Serbo-Croatian and my lack of financial funding, I was poorly equipped to carry out serious fieldwork among Yugoslav Gypsies. Despite these real limitations I spent a month in Zagreb observing Gypsies in public places, almost all of whom were engaged in three major economic activities with non-Gypsies: begging at the train station, shining shoes, and selling shish kebabs on busy streets. At night, Yugoslavs who had befriended me took me to the areas of the city where the Gypsies lived, and I observed them at a distance. Upon returning from Yugoslavia I began my graduate studies at the University of California, Los Angeles, where I embarked on a nine-year study of American Gypsies that has resulted in this book.

The People

The intriguing thing about Gypsies in the United States is that everyone has seen them, but nobody knows them. I call Gypsies familiar strangers because they are both familiar and strange; Gypsies probably live in your hometown or city, or you may have a vivid childhood memory of them, yet you cannot say you really know them.

This distance between the Gypsies and us has been intentionally created by both sides. The Gypsies worry us, given their nonconformity and negative stereotypes: they kidnap children, steal anything in sight, and dabble in the occult. The few curious outsiders who have tried to befriend Gypsies are usually discouraged by them. On the other hand, we worry the Gypsies because we are capable of abuse toward ourselves and toward them. Through their fortunetelling business and the media, Gypsies get a warped view of us; it is hard for them to believe there are well-adjusted *gaje* (non-Gypsies).

While many Americans visit a fortuneteller just once in a lifetime, on a lark, many others seek the advice of fortunetellers on a regular basis. Many of these regular customers are lonely, maladjusted, or both. They reveal aspects of *gaje* life to the fortuneteller which sound deviant to her; in turn, she tells her family everything she has heard. Based on what the fortunetellers hear in their parlors, it is difficult to convince them that there are non-Gypsies who do not commit incest, adultery, homicide, unethical business practices, or a myriad of other antisocial behaviors.

The media, in the form of television and movies, reinforce the Gypsies' view of us. The *gaje* on the screen cannot resist any urge or temptation. They are reckless and undisciplined; extramarital sex and violence abound. News programs reveal that we abuse our children, discard our elderly, and do not provide shelter and food for the homeless and hungry. To the Gypsies we seem cold, selfish, and violent. Thus they have stereotypes about us. No wonder they keep their distance.

While there are no hard demographic data on the Gypsies, Gypsy leaders believe that there are about one million Gypsies living in the United States.[1] This large number may startle some readers, but if you investigate the possibility yourself, you will notice that almost every American city, town, and rural village has a Gypsy community.

The largest concentrations of Gypsies are in major urban areas such as Los Angeles, San Francisco, New York, Chicago, Boston, Atlanta, Dallas, Houston, Seattle, and Portland. But it is an unfounded myth, often perpetuated by anthropologists and journalists, that Gypsies are exclusively urban; in fact, probably half of the total United States Gypsy population is rural. I have found rural Gypsy fortunetellers not only in California and Virginia, where my field-work was concentrated, but in rural Alabama, Mississippi, Georgia, North Carolina, South Carolina, Texas, Arizona, Utah, Nevada, Idaho, and Minnesota. The Gypsies deliberately space themselves geographically because they practice a strict form of economic ter-ritoriality necessary for survival (see chapter 6).

Another demographic misconception about Gypsies is that their largest population is concentrated in eastern Europe. Actual esti-mates for the Gypsy populations in Hungary and Czechoslovakia range from 200,000 to 300,000 (Schechtman 1966:59; Ulč 1972:139; McDowell 1970:97; Guy 1975b:6); these figures are roughly equiv-alent to the number of Gypsies living in California alone (Dean 1986:1).[2]

Gypsies live in about forty different countries, with an estimated world Gypsy population between eight and ten million. Precise numbers on Gypsies are difficult to obtain because of their distrust of outsiders, whom they fear will later use the data against them in some way.

From the Gypsies' point of view, they like being familiar strang-ers. Since all Gypsy business endeavors seek non-Gypsy customers, they need a degree of familiarity with us to earn a livelihood. They also enjoy the option of procuring services from us which they can-not provide for themselves, such as medical and dental care. More-over, their status as strangers protects them in a number of ways. The less we know about them, the less we can harass them. In the United States, Gypsies are not systematically recognized by any branch of the government; consequently they are free to be them-selves, unlike their European counterparts, who are either targeted by various governments for special programs to aid in their assimi-lation into society or subjected to laws restricting their camping rights, length of residence, and general movements.

METHODOLOGY

Fieldwork

Without my background and the relationship I had developed with Los Angeles Gypsies, I could never have succeeded in this study. The

Gypsy world is largely closed to non-Gypsies, but I gained access to many aspects of Gypsy life through a family relationship based upon years of positive personal and business dealings and mutual trust.

During the course of my fieldwork my presence was never obvious to outsiders. I look like a Gypsy myself, and when I was conducting fieldwork I dressed in accordance with Gypsy tradition, wearing midcalf-length dresses or skirts and occasionally a *diklo* (a scarf which covers the hair to distinguish a married woman). I learned a form of body language and an interactional style which Gypsies use in dealing with non-Gypsies. My physical appearance was a definite asset in conducting my research.

My richest fieldwork data were collected in the Los Angeles area because of my long-term contacts. The majority of my informants were Kalderash Gypsies, although I also had some Machwaya informants. My Los Angeles informants provided introductions and recommendations to Gypsies living in other parts of California; thus, I was able to carry out fieldwork in two rural central California cities and in three California coastal towns. My site of fieldwork was usually fortunetelling parlors, the hub of daily Gypsy life. Since Gypsies typically live behind their fortunetelling parlor, business and home life are constantly merged.

There were other sites for fieldwork. I accompanied Gypsies to welfare offices while they arranged for benefits; again, it was assumed by non-Gypsy social workers that I was another Gypsy. I also went with my Gypsy informants to medical clinics and hospitals. This form of fieldwork was very fruitful as it constantly put me in a situation where I could observe Gypsies interact with non-Gypsies in a variety of crucial interactions.

Another dimension of my fieldwork was interviewing non-Gypsies who had extensive dealings with Gypsies. In this research role I presented myself as a sociology graduate student. I interviewed city attorneys, police chiefs, welfare workers, and health care providers. Often these informants supplied names of others who had dealings with Gypsies and would be interested in sharing information.

In February 1980 I traveled to Virginia to present my research at a sociology conference and to make arrangements for using historical archives and libraries that summer. I had selected Virginia as a focus for the historical part of my study because of the general belief that the first Gypsies in America were deported there from England during colonial times. I wanted to document this belief with historical records. While I was making my arrangements in February I looked up the word "palmist" in the telephone book's yellow pages. I was astounded to find pages of fortunetellers advertising their services. This surprised me since fortunetelling by palmistry or any other method was illegal in California and therefore certainly not advertised in the yellow pages by Gypsies. By calling every fortuneteller listed in the phone book I learned several important things: all these fortunetellers, except two, were Gypsies; fortunetelling was legal in Virginia; and Gypsies enjoyed the freedom of operating fortunetelling parlors as lawful enterprises. Through phone books I located fortunetelling parlors throughout rural and urban Virginia, and during that summer I visited almost every one. I purposely excluded fortunetelling parlors in the suburbs of Washington, D.C., because I did not think they represented Gypsy life in Virginia.

In each town where I visited a fortunetelling establishment I tried to interview non-Gypsies who had contact with the fortuneteller and her extended family. In these small towns, police chiefs and city attorneys were often very cooperative. Other townspeople, in no particular position of authority, were also happy to talk about the Gypsies in town.

Gaining entry into the Gypsy community of Virginia was difficult because I did not have the contacts I had in California. Since the Virginia Gypsies were uncertain of my motives, they kept me at a distance. Almost all of my observations took place in the front part of the fortunetelling parlors where outsiders were allowed.

Ultimately this imposed distance forced me to look at the group in different ways than I had in California. Through this fieldwork in Virginia I gradually learned that Gypsies practice a very strict form of economic territoriality, strategically spacing their fortunetelling parlors and other economic activities at geographical distances safely protecting them from the competition of other Gypsies. I realize now that if I had enjoyed closer contact with the Virginia Gypsies, my view of Gypsy life would have been more myopic. Immersed in the daily and celebratory lives of a few extended families in one city, I would never have seen the larger picture.

In the fall of 1980 I traveled to Great Britain in an attempt to gather some comparative data. Because I did not have any contacts with the British Gypsy communities, I had to rely on the same approach I used in Virginia. By focusing on fortunetelling establishments, I visited a number of cities along the southern coast of England and in Wales. Like their American coethnics, I found that English and Welsh Gypsies strategically spaced their fortunetelling parlors to avoid competition with other Gypsies. The English cities in which I could document this practice were Brighton, Portsmouth, Southhampton, Bournemouth, Liverpool, and Chester; in Wales I observed the same strategy in Cardiff, Swansea, Carnarvon, Aberystwith, Ilanelly, and Bangor.

Historical and Comparative Dimensions

In researching the historical and comparative aspects of this book I traveled to many libraries and archives in addition to the UCLA Research Library.

During my stay in Virginia I gleaned information from libraries and archives in Richmond and Williamsburg: in Richmond, at the Virginia State Library and the Virginia Historical Society; in Williamsburg, at the College of William and Mary's Institute of Early American History and Culture and its Law Library and the Colonial Williamsburg Historical Research Department. At both the Institute of Early American History and Culture and the Colonial Williamsburg Historical Research Department, I was extremely fortunate to have the expert assistance of a number of colonial-period historians. My research has benefited greatly from their interest and willingness to help me in my project.

While I was in Great Britain, I made use of the libraries at London University, London School of Economics, and the R. A. Scott Macfie Collection on Gypsies in Liverpool. I gathered additional source data at the Weybright Archives of Gypsies in New York and the main branch of the New York Public Library.

OTHER STUDIES

Until 1975 very little social science research was published on Gypsies in the United States. The only prior significant article was published in 1936 by Erdmann Doane Beynon (1936:358–70), a sociologist who became interested in Gypsies while studying Hungarian immigrants in Detroit. Viewing the Gypsy community as an appendage of the Hungarian community, Beynon observed that most of the Gypsies were musicians who earned a living by playing at religious and secular festivities held in the newborn Hungarian-American community. He believed that the Hungarian Gypsies followed their non-Gypsy counterparts to America to earn a living doing what they had done in Hungary.

In his analysis Beynon described the Gypsies' economic survival as that of a pariah group totally dependent on the musical needs of the Hungarian community and intent on earning a livelihood from a familiar host. Since non-Gypsy Hungarian orchestras were undercutting the Gypsies, he was skeptical about the Gypsies' future in the United States. He viewed these pariah immigrants as mono-occupational, in continuous peril of losing their single occupation due to competition.

The strength of Beynon's study is his observation of and personal contact with the Detroit Gypsies. To obtain information he conducted a house-to-house canvass of the Gypsy community. From his survey he gleaned some interesting but simplistic information about how Gypsy musicians survived financially in a competitive and modernizing Detroit. What Beynon's study lacks is any attempt to compare the Detroit Gypsy musicians with Gypsies in other parts of America or elsewhere in the world. It is clear that he saw the Detroit Gypsies solely as a pariah group totally dependent on the whims of the Hungarians.

Rena C. Gropper's book, *Gypsies in the City* (1975), is an anthropologist's report of one extended Gypsy family in New York City, based on participant observation and ethnographic fieldwork data. While much of the book provides lively and rich observations, Gropper makes no attempt to compare the Gypsies she has studied with Gypsies in other parts of the United States or the world; she simply assumes that all Gypsies are alike. For example, because the Gypsies Gropper studied in New York are urban, she concludes that all Gypsies are urban. Gropper's study lacks a conceptual framework to explain the Gypsies' cultural and economic survival in a hostile world.

Anne Sutherland's article and book, both entitled "Gypsies: The Hidden Americans" (1975a and 1975b), represent perhaps the best anthropological accounts of Gypsy life in America. To collect the information for these works, Sutherland spent nine months as the principal of and teacher at the Barvale, California, Gypsy School, funded by both the local welfare department and the Children's Hospital of San Francisco.

The strength of Sutherland's work comes from her talent and ability as an ethnographic fieldworker. She meticulously observed, interviewed, and recorded all the details she could about the Gypsy community in Barvale. Unlike Gropper, Sutherland paid careful attention to the dynamics and maintenance of insider-outsider boundaries by the Gypsies. Sutherland's discussion and analysis of the tensions existing between Gypsies and non-Gypsies in the world of the welfare department are exceptional.

Sutherland's most interesting contribution is her examination of how Gypsies use the prejudices and negative expectations of non-Gypsies to get what they want. In "Economic Relations," chapter 3 of *Gypsies: The Hidden Americans*, Sutherland explains how Gypsy men collect welfare by intentionally failing IQ tests which label them too mentally retarded either to work or be trained in any occupation. For example, psychologists at the welfare department determined that one Gypsy man had an IQ of 64, with a mental age of about ten years. Later this same man told Sutherland: "The trick is never to protest anything, but act like you are doing everything right and are, you know, simple-minded and good-hearted about it. Anything she asks me I just give some wrong answer" (Sutherland 1975b:81). This is just one example from the many Sutherland uses in her book to illustrate the constant tug-of-war between Gypsies and non-Gypsies.

Sutherland's major weakness is her narrow focus; like Gropper, she examines only one Gypsy group in one brief time period and makes no attempt to compare the Barvale Gypsies with other Gypsies living in the United States or other similar ethnic groups. Her study is purely descriptive and lacks any theoretical framework upon which hypotheses can be tested. Sutherland admits this weakness, stating in her introduction (p. 9) that a comparative study of several Gypsy groups is necessary, but she rightly claims her work as a step in the right direction.

Gypsies, Tinkers and Other Travellers, another important book published in 1975, was edited by Farnham Rehfisch. While all of the selected essays on Gypsies and other traveling groups make serious contributions, I found the pieces by Carol Miller and Teresa San Roman most valuable. Miller's essay brilliantly describes and analyzes the Gypsies' belief and practice of *marime* or symbolic purity. Although her essay focuses on American Gypsies, I am sure scholars studying Gypsies in other societies will find it highly revealing. The essay by San Roman, an in-depth look at Gypsies in urban Spain, studies how Gypsies maintain their social and economic order in a non-Gypsy society and provides a sensitive view into the Gypsies' legal system and sense of justice.

Gypsies and Government Policy in England (1975) by Adams, Okely, Morgan, and Smith provides a thorough understanding of Gypsy life in England by focusing on the Gypsies' struggle to gain the right to camp on government-approved sites. The book, extremely rich in fieldwork observation, examines the laws and policies which have discriminated against Gypsies in England.

Building on the ecological model of competition developed by Barth (1955) and Hannan (1979), Lauwagie (1979:332) asserts that the Gypsies endure through strategies as varied as discovering new sources of income, organizing rapidly to exploit new resources, dispersing quickly in search of new resources, and maintaining a very high birth rate to exploit any economic niche. Lauwagie is both right and wrong. While the argument that Gypsies survive successfully by discovering and rapidly exploiting new resources seems true, the evidence does not support the undocumented claim that they are "prolific" (p. 331) and therefore more able than their less prolific competitors to exploit a particular niche. Lauwagie contradicts herself: she claims on one hand that rates of intermarriage and assimilation among the Gypsies are surprisingly low (p. 328), while on the other hand she states that "the high birth rates, together with some marriage into the group, imply a significant amount of passing into the general population. Otherwise, the Gypsy population should have grown far beyond its present state" (Lauwagie 1979:331). Lauwagie appears unaware that Gypsies practice birth control and limit the size of their families as carefully as any of their white middle-class counterparts in the United States and western Europe. For the Barth-Hannan model to explain accurately the survival of Gypsies, it seems necessary that they meet all of the model's theoretical features. In the case of the Gypsies, wrongly lumped together with Irish travelers and other nomadic groups, the theoretical fit is poor.

Most recently Judith Okely, a social anthropologist, has made a significant contribution to the study of Gypsies in her book *The Traveller—Gypsies* (1983). Okely has focused her study on Gypsies living in camps between 1971 and 1975 in Great Britain. In order to do her research, Okely had to gain entry on two levels. First, she had to convince a warden to allow her to live in a Gypsy encampment. After obtaining permission from a sympathetic warden, Okely set up life in a trailer, working as a "student helper." Entry at the second level of the Gypsy community was far more difficult. In order to accomplish this task, Okely chose to abandon her usual clothing for modest long skirts and high-necked sweaters. She learned to imitate the Gypsy pronunciation of English words and peppered her conversations with their argot.

Firmly believing that sheer observation is too passive an ethnographic style, Okely became as active a participant in Gypsy life as possible. One important way she made inroads into the Gypsy community was to participate in economic production. Okely acquired a van and went calling for scrap metal with two Gypsy women. As the collection and salvage of scrap metal figures importantly in the economic sphere of English Gypsies, Okely began to be perceived as competent and useful by the community. Having thus collected a massive amoung of data through her fieldwork, historical accounts, government records, and popular press articles, Okely has analyzed English Gypsy internal life and the life they share with dominant society. Okely's most important contributions in the book deal with the Gypsies' economic survival, their maintenance of symbolic boundaries, and the status of women.

I have benefited enormously from the other studies done by social scientists. Many of these recent works have provided considerable information and analysis. The works on Gypsies outside of the United States have given me a wonderful opportunity for comparative analysis. While I draw on the research of other social scientists to compare, contrast, and validate my findings, I also hope to advance the literature on Gypsies with new data and alternative ways of looking at them as an ethnic group.

ANALYSIS AND THEORETICAL ORIENTATION

In writing this book I wanted to go beyond merely describing my ethnographic observations and revealing the comparative and historical facts I uncovered. I wanted to write about American Gypsies in a conceptual way to help scholars and general readers view Gypsies as a distinct ethnic group. As a sociologist I am motivated to understand how Gypsies function as a minority group in our society. Thus, I looked for similarities and patterns among Gypsies in the United States and Gypsies in other countries and was forced to make conceptual sense out of the differences.

The anthropologist immerses himself or herself in the life of the community being studied, yielding incredibly vital and rich information, information that can be obtained in no other way. As a sociologist I have borrowed the methodology of anthropology by conducting fieldwork, but I have coupled this approach with the investigation of a voluminous amount of historical and comparative data. This marriage of methodologies has given me a near and far perspective on Gypsies: simultaneously a microanalysis of daily American Gypsy life and a global understanding of the ethnic group.

The Gypsies pose many contradictions for the social scientist. To analyze the Gypsies' status in America and the larger world I have used a recently advanced sociological theory, middleman minority theory. This theory—advanced by Blalock (1967), Bonacich (1973, 1974), Bonacich and Modell (1980), Light (1972, 1977, 1979), and Zenner (1976)—has been applied to a number of minority groups in the middle economic, social, and political strata like the Jews, Chinese, Japanese, and Armenians. I selected this theoretical framework because I thought it could not only explain many issues raised by Gypsies as a minority group but also refine the theory itself.

The overriding theoretical question this study poses is why the Gypsies have not been assimilated into the greater society. *Familiar Strangers* seeks to elucidate both the internal and external mechanisms working to prevent assimilation and attempts to analyze the Gypsies as a middleman minority in the United States. Chapter 2 provides an in-depth discussion and review of middleman minority theory literature, illuminating many unresolved issues in this area. Chapter 3 explores Gypsy migrations and expulsions in the Old and New Worlds. Chapter 4 studies the Gypsies' religion and its prevention of assimilation into their host societies. Chapter 5 examines the Gypsy family and kinship structure. Chapter 6 discusses the Gypsy practice of economic territoriality, the system of justice to uphold it, and the use of non-Gypsy officials to help maintain it.

Chapter 7 deals with special economic practices the Gypsies have developed to compete in hostile host environments. And lastly, chapter 8 summarizes Gypsy economic and cultural life and survival.

Chapter 2

MIDDLEMAN MINORITIES

*S*OCIOLOGISTS HAVE long observed and written about ethnic minorities who throughout history have functioned
economically and socially in the middle levels of society.
Max Weber asserted that the European Jews, the first group observed
in this position, were the "most impressive historical example of
pariah people" (1952:3). Weber defined pariah people as a "guest
people who were ritually, formally or factually separated from their
environment" (1952:3). Additionally, he noted that the Jews had
"specific occupational traditions," "belief in the ethnic community," "strict segregation from any avoidable personal intercourse,"
and a "legally precarious situation" (1953:933–34; see also Cahnman 1974:156–57). Owing to their economic indispensability, the
Jews were tolerated, frequently privileged, and lived interspersed in
various political arrangements.

Simmel labeled Jews "strangers" and wrote a highly abstract essay
listing eleven distinctive traits associated with this social type
(1950:403; see also Sway 1981:42). Simmel observed that the
stranger appeared everywhere as a trader, providing his customers
with goods and services that could only have originated outside their
physical setting. The stranger could be more objective in his commercial dealings because he was "not organically connected" to his
customers "through established ties of kinship, locality, and occupation" (Simmel 1950:404). While Simmel cited objectivity as an
advantage for the stranger in trade, he simultaneously recognized
the dangers of "not being organically connected." Agreeing with Weber, Simmel saw the position of the stranger as not only "legally
precarious" but also dangerous (1950:402). The stranger who was
everywhere seldom gained full entry into the political, social, or
military ranks of the elite. When trouble within the greater society
occurred, the stranger was suspected because the dominant group
perceived him as an "inner enemy."

Following Weber and Simmel, sociologists neglected this area of minority relations. In 1967, Hubert M. Blalock's *Toward a Theory of Minority-Group Relations* revived interest in these pariah people and strangers, now currently referred to as middleman minorities. Edna Bonacich (1973) further developed Blalock's theoretical propositions in her important essay on middleman minority theory. Since the contributions of Blalock and Bonacich, the literature on middleman minorities has grown in terms of conceptual understanding, thus enabling scholars to include such diverse groups as the Chinese, Japanese, Armenians, Parsis, Indians, Iraqi Chaldeans, and Gypsies under the same rubric.

THE SOCIAL STRUCTURE AND THE STATUS GAP

Blalock (1967:80) maintained that middleman minorities were most commonly found in peasant-feudal societies. Traditionally these minorities were wedged between a numerically small elite and a large group of peasants, serving both groups as artisans, merchants, and petty officials. Like the earlier thinkers on the subject, Blalock observed that middleman minorities occupied a vulnerable position in this triadic situation, depending on the elite's goodwill or tolerance: "In times of prosperity and reduced class conflict the middleman finds himself relatively secure under the protection of the elite group. In times of stress, however, he becomes a natural scapegoat" (Blalock 1967:81).

Even though these groups have been surrounded by adversity, Blalock (1967:84) noted they were able to develop and perpetuate a cultural heritage involving a high degree of ethnocentrism and adaptive skills which enabled them to improve or maintain their competitive resources. This last observation stimulated others in the field to explore the internal dynamics of these middleman minorities and learn the intricate methods they employ to survive economically and culturally.

> Though it is perhaps true that most minorities are low-status groups, there are some that occupy intermediate positions owing to a competitive advantage or a high adaptive capacity. Such groups are often associated with special occupational niches, plus a cultural heritage that has been used as an adaptive mechanism over a prolonged period. . . .

As long as the social system remains structurally the same, these groups often become "perpetual" minorities, whereas minorities that are initially less fortunate may become completely absorbed into the dominant group (Blalock 1967:79, 84).

An important focal point when studying any middleman minority is to examine the socioeconomic structure of a host society. Many authors have remarked that middleman minorities initially fill a "status gap" in the societies in which they dwell (Blalock 1967:80; Bonacich 1973:583; Rinder 1958:253; Sway 1975:48–49; Zenner 1976:4). Zenner (1976:4) describes the status gap as a circumstance in which a dominant elite is disinclined to enter the commercial sphere, and the indigenous peasantry does not possess the skills necessary to undertake such activities. Usually middleman minorities, ethnically dissimilar from the host populations, are imported or lured to these economic niches by governmental invitation or summons, the promise of exceptional economic opportunity, or situational creativity. Bonacich and Modell contend that "middleman minorities originate in immigration rather than conquest" (1980:15).

Contrary to Blalock's theoretical proposition, careful historical analysis of various middleman minorities reveals that despite major changes in the social structure, these groups remain "perpetual minorities." In an earlier article I demonstrated how Gypsies were able to persist in their middleman niche over a 500-year history despite radical alterations in the social, economic, and political structures of three societies in France, Germany, and the Soviet Union (Sway 1975:48–55).

Bonacich (1973:584) has also commented that middleman minority groups "persist beyond the status gap." Moreover, "these same groups become middlemen wherever they go. Chinese, Indians, Jews in every country show a similar occupational concentration (thus, a status gap in the receiving country cannot explain the pattern). This regularity suggests that culture of origin is an important factor" (Bonacich 1973:588).

Importation into the Status Gap Through Invitation

Thus the Jews immigrated to Poland as a "complementary population" supplying absent skills (Heller 1977:15). They served as intermediaries between lenders and borrowers, since the Roman Catholic Church forbade its members to lend money for interest; later, during the thirteenth and fourteenth centuries, Jews functioned as administrators of the mint and the salt mines. The Jews persisted in Poland for over one thousand years, living under princes and foreign colonizers and as citizens of a free and independent Polish nation created after World War I.

During these transitions, the Jews' grand economic beginnings as bankers and administrators for the elites steadily declined; by 1937 those who had not been forced to emigrate out of sheer poverty were highly concentrated in service and craft occupations. Eitzen (1972:125) estimates that "eighty percent of the tailors, 40 percent of the shoemakers, 25 percent of the butchers and bakers, and 75 percent of the barbers in Poland were Jewish." By 1939, Poland had three million Jews who endured, however pitifully, as middlemen despite internal and external forces which over the millennium had altered Poland's political, economic, and social structure. The Jews still would be a middleman minority in Poland today if Nazi genocide had not killed almost the entire population.

Filling a Status Gap Through Situational Creativity

Another method by which a group can fill a middleman niche is through situational creativity. For example, Loewen described the Chinese in the Mississippi River Delta (1971). The Chinese were first encouraged to come to the Mississippi Delta in the 1870s to work as sharecroppers by white landowners who were eager to replace belligerent, Republican blacks. When the Chinese were illtreated at the hands of the whites, they abandoned sharecropping and opened grocery stores in black areas. The Chinese seized this opportunity that whites ignored because of racist ideology. From the period of Reconstruction through the Great Depression of the 1930s to the present, the Chinese community remains in between the blacks and the whites in Mississippi.

English Gypsies in the West Midlands have also demonstrated situational creativity. For years certain groups of Gypsies worked as seasonal farm labor, picking fruit and hops, until they were squeezed out by immigrants from India and Pakistan. Instead of leaving the area, the Gypsies turned their rivals into "calling" customers. To the Gypsies' surprise and satisfaction, they discovered that these customers were more easily persuaded to buy lace, ribbon, waxed paper flowers, and to have their fortunes told than the indigenous population (Adams et al. 1975:193–94).

In reality, all middleman groups display situational creativity frequently in the course of their sojourn in a host society. The structure of a society is not static, and middlemen are alert to change and its new possibilities. When they are forced out of a niche, they respond with the amazing ability to turn an adverse situation into a profit-making one. The profit may afford only a meager livelihood, or it may be a substantial financial gain.

Blalock's assertion that middlemen only remain middlemen so long as the societal structure remains rigid is misleading and unsubstantiated by other studies. The structure of any society is in a constant state of flux; all societies evolve, some faster than others. However, middleman minorities may be the only groups that can accept change through demonstrated flexibility: they have cultivated a future-time orientation which has enabled them to expect and sense change and adapt accordingly.

There is more evidence to show that the elites and the masses dissolve with the changing social structure, not the middlemen. The themes of déclassé aristocracy and miserable agricultural workers forced into urban areas by industrialization are far more familiar to us than the plight of the disappearing middleman. Theodore Fontane illustrates this paradox in *Effi Briest* (1967) and *Frau Tres Belle* (1979); in these novels, Fontane clearly depicts the turmoil of late nineteenth-century Germany during its transformation from a feudal society to a more complex industrial one. He sardonically portrays the downwardly mobile behavior of the *junkers* (elites) who, through their most desperate efforts to preserve their east Elbian estates and passé lifestyle, marry the daughters of untitled middle-class merchants. Simultaneously, Fontane paints a grim picture of the lives of rural peasants who migrated to the rapidly industrializing cities. Hence, only the middle class, including the Jews, seems prepared for the tumultuous transformation for which they are economically prepared but never socially accepted. Werner Sombart summed up the dilemma of the times: "To marry a capitalist's daughter is to fertilize one's fields" (see Loewenberg 1977:1).

It is possible that the elites and the masses suffer from a "past-time orientation" and lack, for various reasons, the ability to predict and adapt to change. Middleman minorities, on the other hand, possess a cultural tradition composed of social and economic mechanisms for survival that have been perfected through a long history of adversity in varied economic settings.

The Sojourner Debate

Sociologists debate the reasons certain groups maintain this middleman status. Bonacich has suggested that middleman minorities exist as nations within nations because they are sojourners with a strong attachment to an ancestral homeland, intending one day to return to their land of origin (1973:586). But Zenner (1976:13) has strongly challenged this underlying motive for their rootlessness in host societies. The minorities themselves tend to confuse the picture for sociologists by expressing a desire to return to their homeland but not acting upon it. The degree of loyalty or attachment to a homeland differs with each middleman group, but an ambivalent pattern emerges in all of them.

In his study of Chinese laundrymen in America, Siu (1952) grappled with this inconsistency. He observed that the Chinese worker living in America became a peculiar type of marginal man who preferred living in "Chinese colonies" rather than integrate into American life. He worked hard and sent money back to China. Siu cites "movement back and forth" in which the laundrymen visited China long enough to sire children and build up the home village, but they usually returned to America (1952:39). Siu quotes the wife of a laundryman who complained in a letter to her husband: "You promised me to go abroad for only three years, but you have stayed there nearly thirty years now" (1952:35–36). Eventually the laundrymen became involved in their American Chinatowns, joining fellow clansmen in benevolent societies which sent proceeds to their home village (Siu 1952:40). Siu found many laundrymen at the end of their years indifferent to returning to China although they had the wherewithal to do so. Therefore, this enigma left Siu to conclude: "The sojourner may make several trips back and forth, he may make only one trip, or he may not make any trip at all. Nevertheless, those who do not make the trip may remain unassimilated just as much as those who do make it. Psychologically the sojourner is a potential wanderer, as Simmel puts it, "who has not quite gotten over the freedom of coming and going" (1952:43).

The case of the Gypsies can assist the sociologist with the sojourning debate because they are an ideal example of a group that sojourns but never intends to return to their native land. The Gypsies left India twelve hundred years ago, and, while they carry with them a strong heritage developed in that country, they express no desire (not even figurative) to return there. Their Indian connections are so weak at this point in history, few Gypsies realize that they are from India. In fact, in 1933 at the first International Conference on Gypsy Affairs held in Bucharest, Romania, the United Gypsies of Europe asked for a piece of land in Bucharest where Gypsies in trouble could settle (Haley 1934:182–90). Later in 1937, Janus Kwiek, the "Gypsy King of Poland," asked Mussolini to grant the Gypsies a strip of land in Abyssinia (present-day Ethiopia) so they might escape persecution in various host societies (see Soller 1938:72; Sway 1975:53).

The Jews are another group which has demonstrated ambivalence toward a return to its homeland. The promise "Next year in Jerusalem" has concluded the Passover seder for over two thousand years, but it has not been practically fulfilled now that the state of Israel exists. Ashkenazic Jews are not fleeing their Diaspora homes to settle in Israel; instead, the opposite is occurring—Israel works hard not to lose more Jews than it gains each year.

There are many possible explanations for this phenomenon. The Jews, having lived in the Diaspora for two thousand years, have had no control over the fate of their homeland economically, militarily, or politically. Until 1948, when Israel was established, "Next year in Jerusalem" was a dream that would only be realized with the coming of the Messiah. The Jews managed the best they could as *Kol Israel* (voice of Israel) in the Diaspora. They maintained a sense of "peoplehood" which existed before and was nurtured after they were dispersed (Light 1972:5). Over time, life in the Diaspora communities became a viable substitute for the ancestral homeland. These communities, despite external abuse, developed unique traditions and institutions. It is not surprising that after two thousand years, a Jew from Iran has very little in common with a Jew from Poland.

Ironically, many ultraorthodox Jewish sects do not recognize the state of Israel and distrust the standards of education and family life established by irreligious Zionists. To many ultraorthodox Jews New York is a more holy city than Tel Aviv. Consequently, an orthodox Ashkenazi family in the United States would be more likely to send their children to school in New York, where they can find suitable spouses, than they would to Israel. Similarly, Syrian Jews living in the United States would search the town of Deal, New Jersey, for a potential spouse for their child before they would consider looking in Israel (Eisenberg 1979:37–40). Not only do the ultraorthodox Jews find it more comfortable to live in the Diaspora, but other segments of the world Jewish community also respond in kind. There is difficulty relating to those in the homeland both personally and communally. Given the passage of so much time, Israel emerges as a collage of many subethnic groups who wish that everyone else in the country would start "acting Jewish."

The Double-Stranger Syndrome

Ultimately, the sojourner becomes a stranger in his or her own land. This is the other side of the middleman minority problem. Members often feel more comfortable in their diasporic communities which reflect the changes their particular group has undergone through their wandering. Middlemen may become too international or cosmopolitan for the provincials back home, or perhaps the homeland can no longer be idealized because it has become too industrial (e.g., Korea and Japan). A "double-stranger" syndrome emerges in which members of a middleman minority do not feel completely at ease either in the Diaspora or in their land of origin. Through their years of wandering they become victims of a type of "double jeopardy," in which they become the extreme form of Stonequist's "marginal man" (1961:80).

Historically, these sojourners may have intended to return to their lands, but, after many generations and even centuries, the idea becomes a weak link with the past. Economically, it is infeasible. Middlemen have only survived in the Diaspora by developing special trades and occupations which often took generations to build. Advantages like the dual ethic, which has helped middlemen succeed, become meaningless in the homeland. Additionally, middlemen may have established businesses, even monopolies, dependent on a complicated network of Diaspora connections unavailable to them in the homeland. Moreover, the homeland economy may be too underdeveloped or overdeveloped for a particular middleman endeavor, making those businesses ineffective there.

Eventually home in the Diaspora becomes a strong contender for the homeland in the hearts, minds, and pocketbooks of the middlemen. In the last analysis, middlemen arrive in their host setting as sojourners but remain as strangers. They are Simmel's potential wanderers "who come today and stay tomorrow" (1950:402).

CULTURAL ASPECTS OF MIDDLEMAN MINORITIES

Behind the endurance of middleman minorities the most potent force appears to be a cultural heritage coupled with the groups' fierce determination to preserve it. Although most authors on the topic have listed the common cultural traits of these groups (Bonacich 1973:585; Eitzen 1972:130–31; Zenner 1976:8–11), this literature still lacks a sense of order or chronology concerning the traits' evolution to form a cohesive bond within the groups.

It is instructive to look at the basic motivating factors that lead middleman groups to establish and maintain separate and distinct communities within host societies. In the case of the Jews, cultural separation follows this pattern:

1. There is a basic, often "divinely inspired" philosophy which draws boundaries between the in-group and the out-group and dictates that the in-group remain a nation apart (this precedes sojourning).
2. The group remains separate by keeping members isolated through residential self-segregation and laws which forbid social intercourse with the out-group.
3. Through extensive social and communal organizations which regulate every phase of the groups' life, the community strives to become socially self-sufficient, requiring contact with the out-group only for economic reasons.

Further research should be done to learn if the cultures of other middleman minorities evolve in a similar way.

The Case of the Jews

The belief that Jews should remain a separate people is a basic theological precept: they should be a light to the other nations and an example of the kingdom of God on earth. Since Jews are both a religious and an ethnic group, the laws governing their religious life cannot be separated from the laws governing other aspects of their social life as an ethnic minority. A strong philosophy of separation between Jews and all others was established along with a code of laws and rituals intentionally designed to regulate the personal and communal lifestyle of this group.

According to Herford (1969:40), rabbis in ancient Israel recorded the oral teachings of the Fathers in Pirke Aboth (ethics of the Talmud; sayings of the Fathers), also called the Mishnah. An examination of some of these early tractates exposes the attitude of the wise in dealing with members of the out-group. By this time the Jews had already experienced living among others, in Persia and Egypt, and as a colonized people living under the rule of Greeks, Syrians, and Romans. In reference to the Romans, Rabbi Gamliel said: "Be cautious with the government for they do not make advances to a man except for their own need. They seem like friends in the hour of their advantage, but they do not stand by a man in the hour of his adversity" (Herford 1969:43). Another Mishnah from Shemaiah states: "Love work and hate mastery and make not thyself known to the government" (Herford 1969:30). From these sayings we can detect an early attitude about self-preservation among Jews forced to live and work among outsiders. These notions accompanied the Jews in their long sojourns away from Israel. Philosophically they were committed to remaining separate; practically it was feasible because they traveled and settled as totally self-sufficient nations. The only thing they needed from the out-group was tolerance and the opportunity to earn a living.

To keep Jews socially isolated from members of the host society, residential self-segregation was essential along with thousands of laws, rituals, and superstitions. Obvious religious practices like the observance of the Sabbath created lines of demarcation. Original *kashrut* (kosher) laws were elaborated and amended by rabbinic laws which further limited social intercourse between Jews and non-Jews. For example, a Jew could not eat food prepared by a non-Jew even if the non-Jew used strictly kosher food and cooking utensils, and, in some areas of Europe, the social drinking of whiskey with non-Jews was forbidden. Stringent laws of family purity, *taharath hamishpachah*, made sexual intercourse with a non-Jewish woman a source of defilement, as all non-Jewish women were classified as *nidas* or ritually impure (Kitov 1974:150–75).

Jews also distinguished themselves from others by their dress. *Sha'atnaz* laws, those laws forbidding the wearing of linen and wool together, would alert a Jew to an individual's religious status. Dress codes also served the internal social order by allowing one to determine a person's marital status at a glance. Later in Jewish history, dress became more important as an intraethnic classification. Even today in the Hassidic community of Williamsburg, New York, clothing, hairstyles, and headcoverings reveal which *rebbe* (rabbi) a person follows.

Many of the laws separating Jews from non-Jews appear excessively strict; the severity of the laws follows the philosophical lines of the very first Mishnah: "Be deliberate in judging, and raise up many disciples, and make a hedge for the Torah" (Herford 1969:19). This idea of "making a hedge for the Torah" is a philosophical device whereby the rabbis built concentric circles of lesser laws around a central precept to serve as a series of warnings to their followers. One would be unlikely "to jump the hedge" and make a serious transgression if he or she were dutiful in maintaining the lesser laws (Herford 1969:21).

Historically, the above-mentioned methods of isolation were buttressed by communal organizations developed to cope with every problem or joy posed by life. Extensive educational systems were built to continue the study of Judaism in the Diaspora. The *Beth Din* (House of Justice) operated and enforced all the laws. Furthermore, strong extended families and kinship networks enhanced these systems. Given all these measures, Jews in the Diaspora successfully prevented assimilation into the host society.

Economic Aspects of Middleman Minorities

Owing to their commitment to cultural separation, it is not surprising that middlemen operate upon a dual ethnic when dealing with members of the out-group in economic matters. As Simmel

(1950:12) noted, strangers are not "organically connected" to their customers, which gives them the freedom to be objective in the marketplace.

One chief feature of middleman minorities is that they tend to be self-employed in "portable" occupations and professions. Liquidity is a common denominator when looking at the types of businesses middlemen become engaged in (Bonacich 1973:585). Typically they fill economic niches as traders, moneylenders and exchangers, craftsmen, artisans, manufacturers of small or unusual items, and providers of services not commonly found in a particular host society. Often they take jobs that no one else in the society wants. In general, middlemen are willing to take risks; they are creative and can sometimes be found in "semi-legal business endeavors" (Light 1977:464–79). It is not uncommon for middlemen to be forced to give bribes to stay in business because the dominant group has defined their occupational niche illegal (Eitzen 1972:128).

Middlemen are successful in business through the cooperation of the entire extended family. The success of a business is viewed as a family responsibility, and all members are committed to help in some way. Unpaid family labor, including the use of women and children, is common. The elderly or infirm members of the family help with the cooking, other domestic chores, and caring for small children. Thus, the help of the entire family eliminates costs and inconvenience. Middlemen also tend to be thrifty, live frugally, and often reinvest their profits in the business rather than improve their standard of living. Intraethnic assistance like rotating credit (Light 1972:19–44), the division of territories to limit intraethnic competition, local and international contacts, and mutual favors allows middlemen to cut operating costs and gain the competitive edge over the out-group.

As Simmel (1950:12) observed, middlemen are usually "no owners of soil"; historically they do not derive their living from the land. Many authors have remarked that their low participation in agriculture has been the result of oppressive measures enacted by host governments to prevent middlemen from owning land (Eitzen 1972:124; Heller 1977:20; Sway 1975:48). However, since in many unrestricted societies middlemen do not engage in farming, one must seriously question whether middlemen are inclined to be farmers in the first place. Two exceptions to the rule have been observed: Bonacich and Modell (1980) make a case for Japanese truck farmers in the United States, and I have observed that Armenians in Fresno, California, are engaged in farming.

Host Hostility

The final trademark of a middleman minority is that they are victims of host hostility. They incur the ire of both the elites and the masses. If anything remains constant as the social structure changes, it is the hatred directed toward middleman minorities. As Bonacich observed, "If whites and Africans can agree on anything in South Africa, it is their antagonism to the Indians" (1973:590).

During periods of political and economic turmoil, middlemen serve as ideal scapegoats (Blalock 1967:84) for the elites, who leave them unprotected for various reasons. Frequently the elites use middlemen as a buffer. In other circumstances, the elites must flee, allowing no provision for the middlemen closely identified with them during their reign of power; this is the current situation in Iran, where the status of the Jews is becoming increasingly more dangerous since the fall of the Shah Mohammed Reza Pahlavi. Finally, those in power may expel or exterminate middlemen from sheer avarice, setting up a situation where the powerful can confiscate the middleman wealth (e.g., former president of Uganda, Idi Amin).

While some middleman groups may become wealthy and amass fortunes, their money is weak. They seldom have political power and never have military power. With their weak money they try to bribe their way out of dangerous situations; however, this method does not always work. The middleman position is a perilous one, and these groups have become victims of pogroms, expulsion, and genocide. The tragic example of Nazi Germany's treatment of the Jews and the Gypsies during World War II demonstrates how treacherous it can be to occupy this niche in society.

Scholars have attempted to explain the underlying reason for this antipathy toward middlemen. Some authors think hatred develops when middlemen become a competitive, rather than complementary, element in the economy (Andreski 1963:208; Bonacich 1973:587; Eitzen 1972:124–125; Heller 1977: 42–43). Andreski has suggested that hostility and overt acts of aggression can be traced to the percentage of the minority in the total population. He maintains that "harassing a minority of 30 or 40 percent often entails great danger, whereas a minority of 1 or 2 percent (provided that it is not particularly conspicuous for other reasons) can more easily escape the attention of the majority unless it is put into the limelight by organized hostile propaganda" (Andreski 1963:205). This made the Jews of pre-World War II Poland candidates for abuse since they comprised 10 percent of the population at that time. Although Andreski's assertion is correct concerning the Jews in Poland, it cannot explain why Gypsies, usually less than 1 percent of any given population, served as scapegoats so often.

Other authors claim that some middleman groups escape harm altogether. In a response to Bonacich, Stryker (1974:281) claims that the Parsis in India have enjoyed relative calm despite their middleman status. Stryker's comment provokes some interesting questions: When there are a number of middleman minorities in the same society, why are some groups singled out for persecution? If the Parsis are safe (and more research should be conducted to support this), which group is not safe? In the same vein, why were the Armenians singled out for genocide by the Turks during World War I, while the Jews were spared? Probing further, what happened to the Turkish Gypsies during the Armenian massacre?

CONCLUSION

This reexamination of current middleman minority theory reveals a number of hypothetical assumptions that have not become true in reality. Despite Blalock's assertion that the structure of the social system must remain, the cultural separation is coupled with economic behavior so that livelihood and ethnicity become inextricably linked. Yet despite this strong ethnic identity, the middleman group does not want to return to its land of origin. Middlemen are not the sojourners Bonacich believed they were. Middleman minorities often remain in the Diaspora by choice and struggle with what I have termed the "double-stranger" syndrome; they are here to stay but never feel fully accepted.

Ultimately middlemen experience the wrath of the dominant society. But what is the real source of this contempt? Resentment of economic success is usually cited as the main source of this wrath, yet this study demonstrates that middleman populations, like the Jews of pre-World War II Poland, are not always well off economically. Nor does the answer to the antipathy lie in pure percentages. Andreski's belief that a minority population of 10 percent is perceived by the dominant group as threatening cannot be universally applied; if Andreski's assertion were true, Gypsies living in any society over history should have been safe, yet they have continually attracted the hatred of the dominant group like a magnet.

In sum, this study attempts to refine current middleman minority theory so that it can be more readily used by others engaged in the study of both established and new immigrant groups. The dangerous possibilities that Simmel connected with the status of stranger still exist, and many unanswered questions remain about the dynamics of society when middlemen immigrate and settle. More research in this area should provide useful answers.

Chapter 3

MIGRATION, EXPULSION, AND HOST HOSTILITY

GYPSY ORIGINS

THE DISCOVERY that Gypsies originated in India was made by Valyi (1763), Rudiger (1777), and Grellman (1787) in the latter half of the eighteenth century (see Gropper 1975:9). A theology student at Leyden University, Valyi noticed an amazing similarity between the language of the Hungarian Gypsies and that of subcontinent Indians. To investigate the possibility that Gypsies originated in India, Valyi asked three Indian students from Malabar to compile a vocabulary list of one thousand words. This list of words was read to a group of Hungarian Gypsies, who understood almost all of them (Clébert 1967:39; Gropper 1975:1: Sampson 1923:157; Wedeck 1973:243).

Since the revelations of Valyi, Rudiger, and Grellman, scholars have learned that the name Gypsies called themselves, *Rom*, comes from the Sanskrit word *Dom*. Literally translated, *Dom* means "a man of low caste who gains his livelihood by singing and dancing" (Sampson 1923:158). Supporting this conclusion, Block (1939:12) maintains that the most accurate translation of *Dom* is "to resound" and derives from the sound made by a drum. In fact, the first pariahs may have been the *Dom*, as the term originally described a despised people who were hereditary drumbeaters.[1]

Philological evidence of the Gypsies' Indian origin is supported by the group's occupational history. The *Dom* earned their living in ancient India as musicians, dancers, and entertainers of all sorts (Clébert 1967:37; Sampson 1923:160). Additionally, the *Dom* were metalworkers—the only group in ancient India to work with iron, a metal considered dangerous according to Indian religious belief (Brown 1928:171). The *Dom* were never agricultural.

Little is known of the early *Dom* in India except this information about their occupations and the fact that they were untouchables, forbidden entry into temples (Brown 1928:174). Unlike the high-caste Hindus, the *Dom* were carnivorous (Brown 1928:174; Sampson 1923:158; Wedeck 1973:243). The first *Dom* to leave India were sent to Persia as minstrels at the close of the ninth century. The Persian poet Firdausi documented this event, describing the twelve thousand newcomers in his *Shah Nameh* (Book of Kings):

> Behram Gour, a wise and beneficent prince of the Sassanide dynasty, realized that his poor subjects were pining away for lack of amusements. He sought a means of reviving their spirits and of providing some distraction from their hard life. With this in mind he sent a diplomatic mission to Shankal, King of Cambodia and Maharajah of India, and begged him to choose among his subjects and send to him in Persia persons capable by their talents of alleviating the burden of existence and able to spread a charm over the monotony of work. Behram Gour soon assembled twelve thousand itinerant minstrels, men and women, assigned lands to them, supplying them with corn and livestock in order that they should have the wherewithal to live in certain areas which he would designate; and so be able to amuse his people at no cost. At the end of the first year these people had neglected agriculture, consumed the corn seed and found themselves without resources. Behram was angry and commanded that their asses and musical instruments should be taken away, and that they should roam the country and earn their livelihood by singing (Clébert 1967:40).

Linguistic evidence indicates that after one hundred years as the "entertainers of the Persian peasantry," the *Dom* separated into two major groups and began nomadic life in the tenth century (Sampson 1923:164). For purposes of clarity, Sampson has distinguished these two groups as the Ben Gypsies, who traveled south, and the Phen Gypsies, who traveled northward into Armenia. The Ben Gypsies wandered into Syria, Palestine, and Egypt and spread throughout the Middle East and North Africa (Sampson 1923:165).

Ancestors of the European Gypsies, the Phen Gypsies, traveled from Persia to Armenia some time after the departure of the Ben group. The many Armenian loan words in this branch's dialect suggest that they stayed in Armenia for a long period of time (Sampson 1923:164–66). The language of the *Dom* was strongly influenced by Armenian, and phonetic changes occurred. The "d" sound of many words was exchanged for the Armenian "l" sound; as a consequence, the *Dom* became known as the *Lom* in Armenia (Sampson 1923:165).

In the early eleventh century Armenia was raided by Seljukian[2] and Byzantine soldiers (Sampson 1923:166). These tumultuous raids motivated the *Lom* to move farther north into Byzantine Greece. Because the Gypsies approached Greece from the province of Phrygia, they were believed to be members of a heretical sect called *Atsincan* (Clébert 1967:54; Sampson 1923:167). A Georgian monk of Mount Athos in 1100 recorded the arrival of Atsincani, whom he described as "wizards, famous rogues, and adept in animal poisoning" (Sampson 1923:167). From this association with the term *Atsincani*, the Gypsies became known as the *Tchinghiane* in Turkish, *Zingari* in Italian, *Zincali* in Spanish, *Zigeuner* in German, and *Tzigane* in French (Sampson 1923:167). However, at some point in their journey from Armenia to Greece, the Gypsies began to call themselves the *Rom*,[3] dropping the Armenian "l" in their name for an "r." Correspondingly, their language became known as Romany.[4] Since the Gypsy language has never been written, it has been easily influenced by the sounds of local languages.

Gypsies roamed Greece for a century, earning livelihoods as snake charmers, fortunetellers, and ventriloquists (Clébert 1967:79; Sampson 1923:167). Their appearance was noted in Crete in 1322 (Kenrick and Puxon 1972:15) and on Corfu in 1346 (Clébert 1967:54). As in Armenia, Gypsies absorbed many Greek words into their language. Greek influence in Romany is considerable; Sampson (1923:166) estimates that every European Romany dialect spoken today still contains a substantial number of Greek words. For example, the Romany words for Friday and Sunday and the numerals seven, eight, and nine are all Greek words, and the Romany word for devil is *beng*, derived from the Greek word for frog or toad (Sampson 1923:167).

By the end of the fourteenth century, the Gypsies were widely dispersed throughout the Balkans (Sampson 1923:168). A document from Serbia dated 1348 states that the local authorities forced the Gypsies working there as shoeing-smiths and harnessmakers to pay an annual tribute of forty horseshoes (Block 1939:43). A Bulgarian document reveals that King Ivan Shishman gave the Rila Monastery some villages inhabited by Gypsies as early as 1378 (Kenrick and Puxon 1972:15). And during this century the Gypsies were first entrapped into serfdom in Wallachia (Halliday 1922:163; Sampson 1923:168).

Gypsy Immigration to Europe

The immigration of the Gypsies to western Europe began in the fifteenth century. Coupled with the threat of the Turkish menace, the inhospitality of the Balkans caused a band of three hundred Gypsies to explore more western regions. This exploration led the Gypsies as far as the Hanseatic towns (Bataillard 1889:186). Promising reports given by these pioneering Gypsies inspired massive Gypsy migrations into northern, central, and southern Europe.

During the following one hundred years, the appearance of Gypsies was documented in virtually every European country (Sampson 1923:168). The *Rom* were reported in the regions of Transylvania, Moldavia, and the Elbe in 1417 (Clébert 1967:54). In 1418, Gypsies were spotted in Leipzig, Frankfurt, Switzerland, and Bavaria; France and Provence in 1419; Flanders and Denmark in 1420; Bologna and Rome in 1422 (Sampson 1923:168). By 1430, the Gypsies were dispersed throughout England, Wales, Scotland, and Ireland. Barcelona saw its first *Rom* in 1447, and the year 1500 marks the Gypsies' appearance in Russia, Poland, and Sweden (Clébert 1967:55).

The advent of the Gypsies in Europe provoked the suspicions of the elites, masses, and the Catholic Church for a number of reasons. The Gypsies approached Europe from the Turkish-occupied lands during a period when the threat of Ottoman domination was real (Maximoff 1946:105). The fact that the Gypsies were dark, strangely dressed, and spoke a language believed to be "a kind of a gibberish used to deceive others" lent credence to the fear that they were spies for the Turks and enemies of Christendom (Guy 1975a:206; Kenrick and Puxon 1972:20). Additionally, misconduct by other wandering bands of beggars, ex-soldiers, and truants caused the settled populations to fear any group of nomads (Kenrick and Puxon 1972:16).

These suspicions soon taught the Gypsies they must assure their hosts that they were Christian travelers and not heathen nomads. To travel safely, it was necessary to have "letters of safe conduct" issued by landed aristocracy or preferably the Catholic Church. As early as 1427 a Gypsy chief, "Duke Michael of Little Egypt," invented an ingenious solution to this problem which was imitated over and over by hundreds of Gypsy chiefs. Duke Michael claimed that he and his followers were on a seven-year pilgrimage in order to repent for denying "the Lord" under the torture of the Saracens:

On Sunday, 17 August, twelve penitents, as they said, came to Paris: there were a duke, a count and ten men, all on horseback, who said they were Christians and natives of Lower Egypt . . . and that it was only a short time ago that they had become so again under the penalty of death. They explained that the Saracens had attacked them, but their faith had weakened. They had not resisted very strongly, had surrendered to the enemy, denied Our Lord, and had become Saracens again.

On this news the Emperor of Germany, the King of Poland and other Christian princes rushed upon their enemies and soon conquered them. They had hoped to remain in those countries, but the Emperor and his allies had held counsel not to allow them there without the consent of the Pope, and had sent them to Rome to see the Holy Father. They all went there, great and small, the latter with great difficulty; and they confessed their sins. The Pope deliberated with his council and gave them as penance that they should roam the earth for seven years without sleeping in a bed. For outlay he ordered that every bishop or crook-bearing abbot should give them, once and for all, ten Tours livres. He then handed them letters patent with these decisions for the prelates concerned, gave them his blessing, and they went on their way (Clébert 1967:61).

For a brief time the impersonation of Egyptian penitents provided the Gypsies with safety and charity. During this period of European Gypsy history, it was common for these "little Egyptians" to camp on land owned by a feudal lord and receive charity in the form of alms and food. During the fifteenth century Gypsies sought alternative sources of income to supplement these charitable donations. Early records mention Gypsies working as horse dealers, fortune-tellers, and petty thieves while accepting the alms (Clébert 1967:59; Foletier 1961; Kenrick and Puxon 1972:16; Trigg 1973:5). In a short time the Gypsies' hosts learned that they had no knowledge of Egypt or Christianity, and the hosts' pity and forgiveness toward their guests became mistrust and hostility. "Thus, Gypsies who came to Tournai, France, in 1431 received money and free wheat; those who came eleven years later were refused entry into the town" (Kenrick and Puxon 1972:16). Once a particular band of Gypsies had worn out their welcome, they moved on with either forged documents or letters of safe conduct issued to them by nobility glad to be rid of them (Winstedt 1932).

The Catholic Church disliked Gypsies because they seemed irreligious, and the Gypsy practice of magic enhanced the Church's image of them as infidels. Fascinated with their ancestral art of prophecy, aristocrats and peasants alike employed Gypsies to tell their fortunes. The Gypsy business of prophecy created competition between the Gypsies and the Church for the superstitious minds of the peasants (Kenrick and Puxon 1972:22).

At first the Church welcomed Gypsies, and Gypsies began to embrace Christianity out of convenience, not faith. Gypsy children were frequently baptized more than once so that extra official documents could be collected to make travel in new territories easier. In the early sixteenth century the Church became convinced these "penitents" were frauds and created conditions that would isolate these alien people from the true believers (Kenrick and Puxon 1972:22). As early as 1456 excommunication became the punishment for having one's fortune told by a Gypsy (Kenrick and Puxon 1972:22; Macfie 1943:66). In 1509 a Catholic priest in Rouen, France, was reprimanded by his superiors for having his palm read by a Gypsy (Foletier, 1961:56). More effective than the policy of excommunication was the assertion by the Catholic Church that the Gypsies were a cursed people partly responsible for the execution of Christ (Kenrick and Puxon 1972:27).

Since both the Church and the European ruling nobility doubted the Gypsies' loyalty as Christians and dutiful subjects, the *Rom* found themselves in a precarious position in European society. Their lack of religious or national allegiance reduced their status to that of perennial outsiders or strangers. It was customary at this time to send foreign beggars back to their birthplace, but no one knew where to send Gypsies. Since it was unlikely that the Gypsies would return to India or any of their former stopping places, they managed as best they could, traveling from one district to another with no real legal status (Van Kappen 1965:54).

Unwilling to work in the agricultural economy, the Gypsies specialized in tasks and occupations that were not in competition with another segment of the settled population. Although highly skilled in metalwork, the Gypsies could not solely depend on this occupation for a livelihood since their entry into craft guilds was forbidden (Kenrick and Puxon 1972:23–24). Consequently, fortunetelling, musical entertainment, itinerant metalworking, patent medicine, and horse dealing became some of the Gypsies' most common occupational niches. As a result, the *Rom* emerged as a middleman minority in European society: intermediate between the dominant elite and the peasant masses, the Gypsies attempted to derive a livelihood from both groups.

Gypsy Immigration to the New World

In less than two hundred years after the Gypsies arrived in western Europe, anti-Gypsy zeal reached dangerous levels. By the close of the seventeenth century, every European country with New World holdings began deporting Gypsies. Although scholars generally believe that the *Rom* first arrived in the New World as deportees from various European countries (Coelho 1892; Foletier 1968:13–22), there has been little historic documentation of this fact. Scholars of American Gypsies claim that the *Rom* were deported from England and France to America during the colonial period (Brown 1922:16; Gropper 1975:17; Hancock 1980:441). It is important to realize that the American colonial period represents a span of three hundred years.

The earliest evidence of Gypsies in colonial America is a 1695 legal proceeding against a woman named Joane Scot, who was tried for the act of illegal fornication. According to Dr. Thaddeus Tate of the Institute of Early American History and Culture,[5] the "act of illegal fornication" during this time period referred to the situation of a woman having a baby out of wedlock. The actual court recording, filed in Henrico County, Virginia, on 1 February 1695, stated: "Joane Scot is discharged from ye p'sentum'ts of the Grand Jury. It being the opinion of this Court that ye Act against ffornication [*sic*] does not touch her (she) being an Egyptian and a non-Christian woman."[6]

Further evidence suggests that not only were the Gypsies living in colonial America, but they also encountered antipathy on the part of colonial settlers. I found two separate entries in the *Virginia Gazette*, the colonial newspaper, which assured the colonials that the "Gypsy problem" was just as bad in England as it was in the colonies. The first entry on 3 March 1768, submitted by a correspondent in Surrey, England, claimed: "Yesterday two traveling gipsies [*sic*] were taken up at Barnes in Surrey, charged with stealing children in that neighborhood and selling them to beggars in Kent Street in Borough." The second entry, published on 2 November 1769, asserted that there were plenty of Gypsies left at home in England, reassuring the colonials that they had not "received them all": "We are assured that there are not less than 5,000 gypsies, vagrants, and smugglers who have taken sanctuary in a wood between Guildford and Naphill. All the farmers and inhabitants thereabouts have suffered more or less from these capacious vagabonds who subsist chiefly by plundering people."

Despite this antipathy, the Gypsies remained and thrived in the Commonwealth of Virginia. In the territory that once was Virginia and West Virginia, Gypsies were legally excluded from the practice of telling fortunes:

> Fortune-tellers, clairvoyants, and practitioners of palmistry and phrenology. Any person who, for compensation, shall pretend to tell fortunes, assume to act as a clairvoyant, or to practice palmistry or phrenology, shall pay an annual State license tax of five hundred dollars for each county or city in which any such business is done. No license issued under this section shall be prorated. Nothing in this section shall be construed as repealing an act approved March thirteenth, nineteen hundred and eighteen, making it unlawful for any company of gypsies or other strolling company of persons to receive compensation or reward for pretending to tell fortunes or to practice any so-called magic art.[7]

The law was not repealed in the state of Virginia until 1930. The new law removed the "anti-Gypsy" clause, making Gypsies equal with anyone else seeking a license to engage in fortunetelling, clairvoyance, palmistry, or phrenology.

Deportation of European Gypsies to the New World seems to have been common. Evidence suggests that England also deported Gypsies to Barbados. According to folklore, the Gypsies intermarried with local Indians and became absorbed into the native population. Additionally, Trigg (1973:12) reports that Gypsies were sent to Australia. Similarly France found the New World a valuable dumping ground for unwanted Gypsies. During the two-year period between 1801 and 1803, Napoleon Bonaparte transported hundreds of Gypsies, mostly men, to Louisiana. However, after Bonaparte sold the Louisiana Territory to President Jefferson in 1803, this deportation plan ceased (Foletier 1968:13–22).[8] Likewise, Spain and Portugal deported their unwanted Gypsies below the equator. During the sixteenth century, Portugal sent hundreds of Gypsies to Brazil (Coelho

1892:79–86). Simultaneously, Spain was deporting Gypsies to its South American colonies (*Journal of the Gypsy Lore Society* 1892:61). These Gypsy deportations from England, France, Portugal, and Spain created the genesis of Gypsy life in the New World.

At this point it is difficult to determine what percentage of the Gypsy population living in the United States today actually descends from those Gypsies deported here during colonial times. Based upon information from my own informants it appears that the majority of American Gypsies descend from immigrants who came to the United States during the large immigration of eastern Europeans in the 1880s and 1890s. In fact, Gypsy immigration followed the same pattern as Jewish immigration to the United States (see Taylor 1971:51–65). Immigration statistics are not available for Gypsies as a separate nationality. Instead Gypsies described themselves as Russians, Poles, Hungarians, or Serbians, citing their country of origin rather than their specific ethnicity.

After the United States passed restrictive immigration legislation in 1924 (Taylor 1971:253), eastern European Gypsies began emigrating to Mexico, Central and South America, and to a lesser extent to countries in the Caribbean basin. Many of these Gypsies and their future families ended up in the United States via this Latin American route. This alternative immigration strategy explains why so many Gypsies living in the United States today speak Spanish and have ties to various Latin American countries.[9]

Legends About Gypsies

Prior to the discovery of the Indian origins of the Gypsies in 1763, many myths and legends were invented to explain the origins and wandering behavior of these mysterious strangers. The Gypsies themselves participated in building these myths either from a desire to confuse non-Gypsies or through actual ignorance.

The earliest legend concerning the Gypsies' beginnings connects them with the crucifixion of Christ. Many variations of this legend have been reported by Gypsies and non-Gypsies alike. The most popular version contends that a Gypsy blacksmith was the only one willing to forge the nails used in the crucifixion of Christ. The blacksmith forged four nails; three nails, taken by the Romans, were used to kill Christ. But the fourth nail resisted any cooling process and continued to burn and sizzle, chasing the Gypsy blacksmith with a vengeance:

> And that nail always appears in the tents of the descendants of the man who forged the nails for the crucifixion of Yeshua ben Miriam. And when the nail appears, the Gypsies run. It is why they move from one place to another. It is why Yeshua ben Miriam was crucified with only three nails, his two feet being drawn together and one nail piercing them. The fourth nail wanders about from one end of the earth to another (Clébert 1967:26).[10]

Another popular myth claiming that Gypsies were Egyptians can be directly attributed to "Duke Michael" and other Gypsy chiefs who claimed to be from a nonexistent country called Little or Lower Egypt. This story was believed to be true by Christians who traced the Gypsies' origins to the Bible. A verse in Ezekiel 39:12 states, "I will scatter the Egyptians among the nations and will disperse them through the countries." This verse was used by Roberts (1830) in his book, *Parallel Miracles; Or, the Jews and the Gypsies,* as biblical evidence that the Gypsies and the Jews were cursed peoples. Acceptance of this myth became wholesale; the *Rom* were known as Egyptians in every European country, and the name Gypsy is directly attributable to this belief. Even Voltaire was convinced of the Egyptian origins of the Gypsies and posited that they were the "degenerate descendants of the priests of Isis mixed with votaries of the Syrian goddess" (Clébert 1967:31).

Less common myths about the Gypsies connect them with the Lost Continent of Atlantis or as descendants of barbaric tribes such as the Huns and the Tartars. In Sweden today, it is still widely believed that the Gypsies are the last remnant of the Tartars and are called *Tattare* (Takman 1976:44).

GYPSIES AND OTHER MIDDLEMEN

The most interesting misconceptions about Gypsies are those which have confused them with other middleman minorities. During various historical periods in Europe and the Middle East, the Gypsies have been believed to be Jews, Armenians, and Chaldeans. Part of this confusion may have stemmed from their appearance: these groups resembled each other but looked different from their hosts. In addition to their exotic physical appearance, these groups were viewed by the dominant populations as strangers, basically landless travelers who could not easily be associated with a familiar country, language, or ruling aristocracy. Periodically these groups have been interwoven, and often they were forced to live near one another on the outskirts of a town. It became natural for them to exchange language and ways of coping in a hostile and dangerous world. In too many tragic cases, the doom of one group meant the doom of another.

The notion that the Gypsies are really Chaldeans probably stems from the fact that the Gypsies did spend some time in the area known as Iraq today. According to Gypsy legend, the Chaldeans were favorable toward them and taught them the science of astrology. In exchange for their hospitality, the Gypsies taught the Chaldeans yoga, how to walk through fire, and other magical feats. Some Gypsy chiefs claim Chaldea as their birthplace, not India. However, philological evidence does not bear this out; in fact, almost no words of Chaldean can be found in the Romany language.

The belief that Gypsies are Armenian is based on the relatively long period of time the *Rom* spent in Armenia on their way to Europe. As pointed out earlier in this chapter, there are many Armenian loan words in the Gypsy language. In Jerusalem today the Gypsies and Armenians live side by side (Torgerson 1980). This may even have been the case in Turkey before World War I where Gypsies were massacred along with the Armenians (Kenrick and Puxon 1972:14).

Common folk and early scholars popularized the idea that the Gypsies were really Jews or perhaps one of the ten lost tribes of Israel. In 1848 a French writer, Colin de Plancy, advanced the notion that the Gypsies were a "race of Jews who had become mixed with Christian vagabonds" (Clébert 1967:33). During medieval times the Jews and Gypsies were accused of bringing the bubonic plague to Europe. They were often forced to live outside of towns, and, as a consequence, Gypsy ghettos are usually next to Jewish ghettos. In Spain, the two groups were forcibly settled together. In the years preceding the Inquisition, which was directed toward the Gypsies with as much venom as it was against the Jews, the two groups exchanged talents and cultures. The most illustrious product of their shared endeavors was Flamenco music. During the Inquisition, a group of Gypsies elected a Jewish leader, Yusef Biboldo, to lead them (Tipler 1968:64); today, the Gypsy name for Jew is still *Biboldo* (Oujevolk 1935:121–27).[11]

Gypsies in Nazi Germany

In modern times the fates of the Gypsies and the Jews have also been linked. During World War II the Nazi's "Final Solution" wedded these two groups again through the plan to rid the Reich of all foreigners. The Gypsies and the Jews were viewed as alien people who warranted a low position on the ladder of racial hierachy. Tracing Germany's thirty thousand Gypsies presented no obstacle for the Nazis, as a Gypsy Information Service had been in existence since 1899 which held the genealogies of nineteen thousand German Gypsies (Schechtman 1966:56). These records were seized in 1936 and used for research concerning "the Gypsy problem" at the newly formed Racial Hygiene and Population Biology Research Unit. Genealogical investigations and interviewing of Gypsies were prompted in 1938 with the issuance of the Decree on the Fight Against the Gypsy Menace.

Once sufficient data had been gathered by the bureau, the racial scientists began proposing solutions for dealing with the "Gypsy Menace." Deportation, segregation, and sterilization were deemed partial solutions for eliminating the Gypsy foreigners. Through policy, each solution became a reality. In July 1936, four hundred Gypsies were transported to Dachau to work at forced labor (Kenrick and Puxon 1972:71). Special residential camps were established for Gypsies between the years of 1933 and 1938 in the Dusseldorf district, near Marzahn, and in the Frankfurt area. By 1938 a strong recommendation for sterilization of Gypsies was under consideration.

The steps taken toward the attempted annihilation of the Gypsy people do not differ from the measures enacted against the Jews during the same period. Restrictive directives issued against the Gypsy minority reduced their status to second-class citizenship even in the years preceding the war. The Settlement Law of October 1939 prevented Gypsies from traveling and forced them to settle in assigned areas (Kenrick and Puxon 1972:75). This measure, strictly enforced, prohibited any Gypsies suspicious of Nazi policies from fleeing. Intermarriage between Gypsies and Germans was forbidden by law, as racial scientists of that time claimed that offspring of such marriages would produce hereditarily tainted persons (Kenrick and Puxon 1972:74). In 1939, Gypsy children were denied the right to be educated.

A memorandum dispatched in 1938 to the Chief of the Chancellery of Austria makes clear the perilous position of the Gypsies and the Reich's intentions toward them: "Because the Gypsies have manifestly a heavily-tainted heredity and because they are inveterate criminals who constitute parasites in the bosom of our people, it is fitting in the first place to watch them closely, to prevent them from reproducing themselves and to subject them to the obligation of forced labour in labour camps" (Kenrick and Puxon 1972:96). The creation of a special department within the Security Central Office headed by Adolf Eichmann became responsible for the deportation of Jews, Gypsies, and Poles. In 1940, twenty-eight hundred Gypsies were transported to Poland from Germany (Levin 1973:432). The deportation of Gypsies from Germany and Axis-occupied territories continued throughout the war. The sadly familiar names of Auschwitz, Ravensbruck, and Bergen-Belsen are as much a part of modern Gypsy history as they are of Jewish history. In October 1939, Eichmann suggested that three or four truckloads of Gypsies be attached to the first transport of Jews leaving Vienna (Schechtman 1966:55). Figuring that this was the simplest method, he proposed its continuation. Thousands of Gypsies were imprisoned in the Birkenau camp near Auschwitz. Following a decree issued by Himmler a special camp designed to hold thousands of people was established within Birkenau for Gypsies (Kenrick and Puxon 1972:152). Starvation and disease were rampant in the camp, and hundreds of Gypsies perished due to the deplorable conditions. In 1944 the Nazis decided the Gypsy camp would be closed and the inmates would be selected either for hard labor, medical experimentation, or death.

On one of the most tragic dates in the history of the *Rom*—1 August 1944—an estimated forty-five hundred Gypsies were murdered in the gas chambers and crematorium. But this is not the only camp where Gypsies were exterminated; Gypsy deaths were also recorded at Chelmno, Treblinka, and Bergen-Belsen.

Medical experiments were performed on Gypsy inmates in various camps. The infamous Dr. Mengele is known to have conducted experiments on Gypsy twins in the children's block of the Gypsy section in Birkenau (Kenrick and Puxon 1972:157). Adult Gypsies were victims of experimentation in which they were forced to consume sea water (Levin 1973:244). Others were exposed to deadly gases, typhus, spotted fever, and underwent sterilization operations without anesthesia (Kenrick and Puxon 1972:177). The catastrophic years of World War II brought the destruction of over a million Gypsies (Maximoff 1946:107; Yates 1949:455). Of course, this number does not give utterance to the misery endured by the Gypsy survivors who were physically impaired and emotionally broken under the Nazi domination.

Persecution of the Gypsies did not end after the Holocaust. Gypsies who survived the camps have had little success in gaining indemnification from the West German government. In trial after trial, Gypsies have been denied reparation for the losses they suffered during the war on the grounds that their internment and suffering was due to their "asocial" behavior and not their ethnicity. Although persons persecuted by reason of nationality were to be compensated under the Bonn Convention, the Bonn government has freed itself from responsibility by claiming that the wartime arrest of Gypsies was strictly on security grounds (*Christian Century* 1971:519).

Today, Germany's Gypsies find leading a nomadic existence difficult because of various forms of legislation prohibiting it. As in France, the Gypsies are regarded as so elusive they must register with the police, who keep them under surveillance (Clébert 1967:257).

CONCLUSION

Originating in India, the Gypsies have become world wanderers. Their nomadism has not been due to wanderlust as much as to pressure exerted upon them by numerous host societies. The original *Dom* who left India in the ninth century were sent as "a gift" to the Shah in Persia. After one year, the Shah encouraged his Gypsies to roam. These twelve thousand Gypsies divided themselves into two groups and traveled in opposite directions: the Ben Gypsies wandered into Syria, Palestine, Egypt, and later throughout northern Africa; the Phen Gypsies adopted a northern route and spread to Europe through Armenia and Byzantine Greece. Often the pace of these migrations was hastened by warfare and violence between conflicting groups at the Gypsies' stopping places.

Despite the suspicious welcomes of their hosts, the Gypsies learned more than one way to earn a livelihood anywhere they traveled. By overcommunicating their strangeness, the Gypsies were able to manipulate various host populations into believing that they were possessors of magical talents. When their clairvoyance was eagerly sought by the masses, the Catholic Church began to perceive them as a threat, and excommunication became the punishment for dealing with Gypsies. After wandering in Europe for two hundred years, the Gypsies were citizens of no country and members of no church. This powerless status made them prime candidates for New World expansion and settlement. Consequently, England, France, Portugal, and Spain deported thousands of Gypsies to the western hemisphere.

In modern times, the older practices of expulsion and deportation gave way to extermination. In the two tragic attempts at genocide in the twentieth century—the first aimed at the Armenians during World War I and the second aimed at the Jews during World War II—the Gypsies shared in the suffering. The Nazi death camps alone killed a million Gypsies.

During their twelve-hundred-year sojourn from India, the Gypsies have endured as landless travelers through the world, subjected to dominant group hostility and violence. Moving from territory to territory, either by desire or force, approximately eight to ten million Gypsies have survived as citizens of the world, living in forty different countries.

Chapter 4

THE GYPSY
RELIGION

🌀HE FUNDAMENTAL force that divides Gypsies from all
other people is their religious belief. Like other middleman minority groups, Gypsies hold the firm religious
conviction that they should remain a separate people. This act of
remaining separate is carefully regulated by a series of intricate laws
known as the *marime* codes among the Gypsies. *Marime* codes gov-
ern every aspect of Gypsy life, from sexual relations between husband and wife to economic dealings with non-Gypsies. They supply
the rationale behind the dual ethic in business dealings with non-
Gypsies. In a sociological sense, *marime* codes safeguard the cohe-
siveness of Gypsy communal life by defining all non-Gypsies as
impure.

Despite the important role religion plays in the endurance of the
Gypsies as an ethnic group, it has received little attention by scholars of Gypsy studies. Brown (1929:163–64), Pickett (1966b:92–95),
Gropper (1975:112), and Sutherland (1975b:256), however, all describe the colorful and occasionally humorous aspects of Gypsy religion, but none of these authors attempts to analyze the function
Gypsy religion serves in maintaining insider-outsider boundaries.
Furthermore, no researcher has tried to determine which aspects of
the religion are authentically Gypsy and which have been adopted
by the Gypsies solely for purposes of protective coloration.

This chapter discusses the sociological importance of the Gypsy
religion in maintaining the separateness of the Gypsy people. It
looks at the ways in which Gypsies have adapted to the pressures of
various host societies by claiming to be Christian. And finally, the
chapter will differentiate between true Gypsy religious belief and
religious camouflage acquired during their twelve-hundred-year sojourn in the world.

RELIGIOUS PRACTICES

Judaism and the Gypsy Religion

The parallels between the Gypsy religion and Judaism are striking. The Gypsies are monotheistic and worship a male god they call *Del* (Gropper 1975:114; Rao 1975:144–47; Sutherland 1975b:255, 275, 285; Wedeck 1973:156). Gypsies, like Jews who observe the second commandment, do not make graven images of their god. Some Gypsies who profess to be Christian will say they accept Jesus Christ as their Savior; however, when I ask them if they believe that Christ is the son of *Del*, they immediately reply negatively. According to Gypsy religious belief, *Del* has no children to worship.

Like the Jews, the Gypsies practice circumcision of their sons (Pickett 1966b:96; Wedeck 1973:156). When I ask Gypsy respondents why they circumcise their sons, the most common answer is "Because we have always done it that way." Either the Gypsies feel it is unsafe for the *gaje* (non-Gypsies) to know the answer to this question, or they honestly do not know any longer. The most they will say regarding circumcision is that it is part of the Gypsy religion.

The Gypsy religion parallels Judaism in another notable way: it is against the dictates of *romania* to kill man or animal. The Gypsies adhere strictly to an anticruelty code which forbids the killing of any living thing, except for the acquisition of food. These anticruelty laws correspond to two of Judaism's Seven Laws of Noah.[1] The Seven Laws of Noah, which apply to Jews and non-Jews alike, are considered the basic rules for human behavior. Two laws— "Thou shalt not murder" and "Thou shalt not eat from an animal while it is alive"—are the Jewish anticruelty laws. The spirit of these laws forbids people from hunting for sport or pleasure (Kolatch 1981:88). The rabbinic interpretation of these laws is that people must not prey on any living thing that is weaker. To destroy a helpless living creature is the ultimate demonstration of cruelty and ungodliness. In fact, according to Rabbi Simcha Wasserman, the former Rosh Yeshiva of Ohr Elcohnon-Chabab in Los Angeles, the most important question a rabbi should ask a person who wishes to convert to Judaism is, "Have you ever hunted animals for pleasure?" If the would-be convert answers in the affirmative, then in Rabbi

Wasserman's opinion, conversion should not be permitted, for this person is considered out of the bounds of humanity.[2]

Jewish *kashrut* (kosher) laws are based upon these anticruelty laws (Kolatch 1981:88–89). According to Jewish law, animals killed for consumption are to be killed by a ritual slaughterer called a *schochet*. It is the solemn responsibility of the *schochet* to kill the animals in the quickest and most painless way possible. Like the Jews, the Gypsies have a *schochet* they call the *masengero* who serves as the ritual slaughterer for the community (Tipler 1968:69). The philosophy behind the use of the ritual slaughterer in each community is the same; both groups do not want their members to become too comfortable killing any living thing. They believe that killing an animal is just one step away from killing a human being.

Like orthodox Jews, the Gypsies believe that one of the major differences between the *gaje* and themselves is the former's lower regard for human and animal life. Gypsies will proudly tell non-Gypsies who will listen to them that, as a group, they have an almost flawless record when it comes to violence against any living thing, including the natural environment, and that they have never been involved in a war, except as victims.

One example of the Gypsies' extreme sensitivity towards living things was revealed when I was interviewing a ten-year-old Gypsy boy. Ants were crawling all over the area where we were talking. When I went to step on the ants, the boy stopped me and said, "Please don't kill them. Ants are good luck to the Gypsies. They really can't hurt us anyway. We can sit somewhere else and let them live." The Manus Gypsies of Germany believe that killing a horse is an impure act and refuse to do it (Rao 1975:154).

Gypsy Belief in Ghosts

Every scholar who has studied Gypsies has reported their belief in and fear of ghosts (Gropper 1975:100–101; Pickett 1966b:85; Sutherland 1975b:274; Tompkins 1971:5; Trigg 1973:46; Yoors 1967:237). Often Gypsies' fear of ghosts is regarded as a childish fear or superstition. However, I think that the Gypsies' belief in ghosts is a religious safeguard that has evolved to prevent Gypsies from committing murder or denying comfort and assistance to the helpless. According to Gypsy belief, if a person dies with feelings of resentment or hostility toward the living, then he or she will return from "the other side" to haunt them. This belief in ghosts is universal among Gypsies. Janet Tompkins, who has worked with Gypsies for years as a social worker, states, "I have never met a Gypsy who does not believe in ghosts" (1971:5).

To avoid visitation from the "other side," Gypsies follow an elaborate set of practices in the event of death. When a Gypsy is hospitalized for any reason other than childbirth, it is believed that he or she is dying. When this occurs, Gypsies near and far are summoned to beg forgiveness from the dying patient. The Gypsies will do anything to prevent death and engage in various methods to ward off evil spirits who threaten to take the patient to "the other side." Tompkins describes the bedside behavior of Gypsies who want to "chase away" the death spirit:

> The death spirit enters the room of a sick person through an open window. He sits on the windowsill, flattering and coaxing, trying to persuade the sick person to follow him to "the other side." A contingent of old women will attempt to drive the death spirit away. They do this by cursing, shaking smoking sticks and, as a last resort, throwing up their skirts and threatening ritual defilement [*marime*] (Tompkins 1971:4).

Similar behavior has been documented in the Yugoslavian short-subject movie, *Dae* (the Romany word for mother), in which a tribe of Skopje Gypsies attempt to drive away the death spirit from a tent in which a woman is undergoing a difficult delivery. A male member of the tribe, perhaps the woman's husband, howls and dances around her tent with smoking sticks, shaking them at some invisible menace. The entire tribe, which has formed a circle around the dancing man and the tent, participate in the ceremony by screaming and shaking their fists. The older women shake their skirts incessantly toward the center of the circle.

Other methods used to frighten away the evil spirits include symbolic transference and symbolic rebirth. These rituals are always performed by the older women of the tribe who have learned how to manipulate the evil spirits from their mothers and grandmothers. For example, illness in newborn babies is attributed to the evil spirit *tsinivari* (Tillhagen 1955:12–13). An unconcerned father can transport *tsinivari* to his newborn baby if he leaves the house after dark during the first six weeks of the child's life. When a newborn Gypsy child becomes ill, he or she is given a new name, but not just any new name will do. The baby must be renamed after an unsavory character like a drunkard or a *gajo* (Tillhagen 1955:13) because Gypsies believe the evil spirits are not interested in taking an undesirable to the "other side." If this "trick" does not fool the evil spirits and the baby's condition worsens, then he or she is sold to another Gypsy for a special sum that reflects some magical numerical meaning (Tillhagen 1955:14). This manipulation of numbers is akin to the Jewish practice of *gematria*.

Pulmonary disease is combated with symbolic transference by having the ailing patient breathe three times into the mouth of a live fish. The fish is then thrown back into running water with the hope that the evil spirits will follow it in confusion (Vesey-FitzGerald 1944:61). To ward off death, herbal medicines and charms are used in combination. The color red is used to counteract the violence of the "evil eye," so most charms surrounding the sick are made of red ribbon or cloth. Often coral necklaces are placed around the patient's neck (Tompkins 1971:7, 9).

The feeling that they must do everything in their power to prevent death explains the psychology behind the Gypsies's recent utilization of non-Gypsy medical services. If non-Gypsy doctors can combat the evil spirits more successfully than the old wise women of the tribe, then it is justified to consort with them. However, if a Gypsy dies under the care of a particular physician, no other Gypsy will ever ask for his or her services (Boles and Boles 1959:56; Tompkins 1971:8).

Death and Gypsy Rites of Mourning

When death does occur despite all of the effort to prevent it, the Gypsies arrange a funeral that will usher the deceased to the "other side" in comfort and style. It is not uncommon for three thousand Gypsies to attend the funeral, and attendance at a *pomana* is mandatory for every Gypsy who knew the deceased. Each visitor goes through the "ritual of forgiveness," in which he or she begs the deceased for forgiveness for any wrongdoing he or she may have committed (Yoors 1967:231). The Gypsies believe that if the deceased leaves this world on good terms with the living, then he or she will not come back to cause any trouble (Yoors 1967:237). For this reason the Gypsies load the coffin with various items to ensure that the deceased has everything he or she needs and wants on the "other side"; then he or she will not be forced to come back to this world for anything (Gropper 1975:171).

It is common for Gypsies to be buried in their favorite outfits. In the case of women, they are buried with much of their jewelry. Money is thrown into the coffin by most of the visitors with comments like, "Here, Jimmy; here's something for a drink on the way" (Vesey-FitzGerald 1973:88; Yoors 1967:235; see also Rao 1975:157–58). Other items like a deck of cards, a favorite pipe, and favorite foods are included. Often Gypsies tell their families while they are alive what they want placed in their coffins when they die. Anna Stevens, a member of the Los Angeles Kalderash tribe, told her children what she wanted to be buried with in order to be content: "I need at least three pounds of Yuban coffee. Don't get me a cheap brand or I'll be real mad at you. And get me a couple cartons of cigarettes—Camel or Benson and Hedges—either one, I don't care."

Observing the rites of mourning is a responsibility that is taken very seriously by the entire extended family of the deceased. After the initial funeral, which lasts three days, the deceased is remembered at different intervals throughout the year in what can be described as a remembrance feast (*pomana*). For the first week after the death, the family must make a *posta* (sacrifice) in which they are not allowed to eat either red meat or poultry. Similarly the food served at the *pomana* is restricted to grains, beans, rice, and fruit. This practice of vegetarianism during periods of grief seems to be universal among the Gypsies (Gropper 1975:108–22; Vesey-FitzGerald 1973:77). Likewise, all tribes mourn for one year, although the intervals of observance differ slightly from tribe to tribe. For example, West Coast Kalderash American Gypsies hold a *pomana* at these intervals: the third, sixth, and ninth days after the death, then at the one-month, six-month, and finally at the one-year anniversaries of the death.[3]

At the *pomana,* two tables are put together in the shape of a "T" or a cross. At the place where the two tables intersect, an ashtray of incense or a single candle is lit both to chase away the spirit of the dead person and to honor him or her (Rao 1975:158). After the *pomana* it is customary to throw all uneaten food into a body of running water. In large urban areas where there is no running water, it has now become common for guests at the *pomana* to take the uneaten food home with them.[4] Members of the immediate family do not take any food home with them since they believe the spirit of the deceased will follow the food and create problems for the family members. At the head of the "cross table" sits a man or a woman selected by the family to play the role of the deceased at the *pomana*. This person is given a brand new suit of clothing, complete with underwear, to wear as a symbolic gesture of respect to the departed. I attended a *pomana* of a man where, in addition to clothing, a bottle of after-shave lotion, a razor, and a coffee mug were added to the clothing as further tributes of respect. The selected guest wears this clothing for a period of three months and then disposes of it, usually by leaving it at a dry cleaner's and never returning.

If all of the rituals of mourning are observed, the Gypsies believe that after one year the ghost of the departed (*mulo*) will be satisfied and not cause any mischief for the living. The Gypsies undergo considerable expense to please the *mulo;* one Gypsy chief told me that he spent $30,000 on the *pomanas* of his departed wife.[5] But the *mule* are fickle beings, and there is no real way of knowing if they are truly content. Discontented *mule* create all havoc, including illness, bad weather, and harassment from the police. When something goes wrong, the Gypsies are convinced that it is the work of ghosts who are seeking revenge. Their fear of ghosts prevents the Gypsies from wishing or causing anyone real harm. While this belief in ghosts is not foolproof, the spirit of the belief constrains pernicious behavior that may lead to someone's misfortune or death.

Gypsies all over North America are still talking about a shoot-out between two feuding families in 1947 in Mexico City during which several people were killed. This incident is regarded as the biggest disgrace in the New World history of the Gypsies. Both sides of the feuding families were tried by the Gypsy court (*kris*) and given *marime* sentences.[6] Now, forty-one years later, some of the families are convinced that they are cursed by the ghosts of that disaster. Indeed, some of the descendants of these families have become increasingly poor over the years and have fallen in both tribal and financial status. During this forty-one-year period, "better" families have refused marriages with them, and consequently their business contacts have dwindled. The older members of the tribe reminisce about the wealth and status they enjoyed in Puerto Rico, Cuba, and

Mexico before the disgrace of the big shoot-out. These Gypsies have convinced themselves that nothing will ever go well for them again because of the *mule* that remain angry at them.

A middle-aged Machwaya woman gave Carol Miller the most accurate statement regarding the Gypsies' basic religious philosophy:

> According to the Rom belief, the attributes of a good life, health, wealth, and happiness, are locked into a clean, and moral family life. Shames join what should not be joined and upset the recognized order of things and events so that calamity visits the family in a form of *Sastimos* (health) reversed, illness, loss of money, bad luck, unhappiness, even death. The most vulnerable to these supernatural sanctions are the children of the familia, the extended family. For these reasons, whenever shames of any size become public knowledge, in order to protect the familia and to stay the tide of unpropitious events, the agent of the shame is labeled as *marime*, dangerous to himself and others (Miller 1975:50–51).

THE GYPSY CONCEPT OF *MARIME*

Another fundamental part of the Gypsy religion is the belief that Gypsies should remain separate from all others. Such separation is maintained by the strict laws of *marime*, which help Gypsies define everything and everyone in the world as *wuzho* (pure) or *marime* (impure or shameful). From a sociological viewpoint, *marime* is the dividing wedge between the Gypsies and all other people; its laws influence every aspect of life, from sexual relations between a husband and wife to financial dealings with the out-group.

A highly complicated concept, *marime* means both pollution and rejection. According to *romania*, the human body is divided at the waist into two halves. The lower half of the body is regarded as *marime* because of the genital and anal areas, sources of pollution. The upper half of the body, regarded as pure and clean, is called *wuzho* in Romany. The head is considered the most *wuzho* part of the human body. Any "co-mingling of the two halves is *marime*" (Sutherland 1975b:258). A Kalderash teenager explained the concept of *marime* to me like this: "The best way I can explain *marime* to someone who is not a Gypsy is like this. You never take a sponge or a wash rag that you use to clean out the bathtub in the kitchen sink. It doesn't matter if you washed it out a million times. It would be *marime* because it touched the tub where your lower body was." At puberty both males and females become subject to *marime* rules. Any violation of these rules is grounds for exclusion from the tribe for the offender and his or her entire extended family; it is the most serious matter Gypsy courts handle.

Marime for Gypsy women is their limitation and their power. Once a woman menstruates, she is considered a source of pollution. She must dress and act in accordance with Gypsy law: the lower half of the body must be carefully covered to the midcalf, and she must sit in a modest position in the company of men, that is, with her legs extended in front of her and crossed (Thompson 1922:22). The Romany word for an immodest sitting position, *pohardi*, indicates not only a shameful form of behavior but also one which exposes adult men to pollution. In public, a Gypsy woman must not allow her skirts to touch adult men, eating utensils, or food (Yoors 1967:150). She must avoid stepping over men's clothing and running water from which men drink (Brown 1929:163–65; Gropper 1975:93–95; Rao 1975:151).

Marime *Rules Governing Marriage, Pregnancy, and Childbirth*

Contrary to the popular stereotype, Gypsies are not sexually promiscuous. In fact, owing to the rules of *marime*, the opposite is true: sexual intercourse between unmarried Gypsies is considered *marime*; sexual intercourse between a Gypsy and a *gajo* is even more *marime*; and even sexual relations between husband and wife are strictly governed by *marime* codes. There is an amazing similarity between the Gypsy laws of *marime* in respect to marriage and the orthodox Jewish laws of family purity, *taharath hamishpachah* (Meiselman 1978:125–29). In fact, the rules for marital sex are almost identical for both groups. The only difference is that the Gypsies have no practice involving a *mikva* (ritual bath) or a monthly return to water (Kolatch 1981:123; Meiselman 1978:126).

Like orthodox Jews, Gypsies are only permitted sexual intercourse when the woman is "pure." Purity is present seven days after the last day of menstrual bleeding till the onset of the next menstrual period (Meiselman 1978:127). Sexual relations during this "pure period" are free, and husband and wife can sleep together in one bed. During times of "impurity," known in Hebrew as *nida* and in Romany as *marime*, husband and wife sleep in separate beds and are not permitted to touch each other in any way (Tillhagen 1955:7). When a Gypsy woman is *marime,* she is not allowed to touch food or eating utensils that adult men will touch (Rao 1975:153; Tillhagen 1955:7). Orthodox Jews have no prohibition when it comes to *nidas* cooking food, but they enforce a similar concept by preventing women from touching the Torah.

During pregnancy, according to both Gypsy and orthodox Jewish laws, women are considered pure. However, after childbirth, both religions regard the mother as "impure" for a period of time (Brown 1929:163). In accordance with the dictates of *marime,* a Gypsy woman must not give birth in her own dwelling. In earlier times, a special tent was erected for the birth process. Once the baby was born, the tent and everything used in the delivery were burned, as these things are regarded as dangerously *marime.* For a while American Gypsies rented special houses for the delivery and mandatory six-week quarantine of the mother and baby; after this, they abandoned the house, and sold all *marime* blankets and other items to the *gaje* (Vesey-FitzGerald 1973:49). Today, the Gypsies feel it is easier and cheaper for a woman to give birth in a hospital, stay as long as possible, and then leave the *gaje* with all the *marime* items.

Direct contact with the genitals is not the only manner in which a person can become defiled. Because any contact with women's underclothes results in *marime,* all women's clothing from the lower half of the body is washed separately (Rao 1975:152; Sutherland 1975b:268). One of my informants told me how appalled she was by the way the *gaje* wash clothes: "I've seen women in the laundromat washing all kinds of clothes together. They don't think nothing [*sic*] of throwing men's and women's underwear in together with dish towels and children's clothes. I think it's disgusting, but I guess they don't know no better." According to the Gypsies, cleanliness is not judged by *how often* something is washed but by *how* it is washed.

Men can also become *marime* indirectly by sitting on a toilet seat that was used by a woman. To avoid this source of *marime,* Gypsies try to rent apartments with two bathrooms—one for postpuberty women and the other for children and men. Some Gypsies refuse to live in a first-floor apartment for fear that a woman will walk over their heads and defile them (Pickett 1966a:12).

Even though the laws of *marime* severely restrict the Gypsy woman, they simultaneously give her ultimate power over men.

Gypsy women have the right to defile any man by an act in which they "toss their skirts" over his head and make him *marime* (Yoors 1967:151). While Gypsy women use their power gingerly, it is their weapon against any kind of abusive treatment from Gypsy men, including rape. Once a man has forced a woman to "toss her skirts," he has brought irreversible disgrace to himself and his entire extended family by acting shamefully and by being defiled (Miller 1975:51–52; Yoors 1967:151).

Violations of Marime

When *marime* codes have been violated, a *kris* is arranged, and the accused is given a complete trial with the testimony of witnesses and evidence. To ensure impartiality, a judge from another *kumpania* is asked to try the case. If the *kris* finds the Gypsy guilty, he is publicly sentenced *marime* and excluded from the tribe temporarily or permanently, depending on the seriousness of the offense. The sentence of *marime* affects not only the guilty party, but also his or her entire extended family. Because *marime* is a moral crime, a "shame" (Miller 1975:50), it becomes a stigma that lingers long after the announced period of exclusion is over. To sum it up, a Gypsy elder told me, "Once you're *marime*, you're out." The following "shames" have resulted in *marime* verdicts in California during the course of my fieldwork: sexual intercourse with a non-Gypsy, rape, incest, beating a member of someone's family, joining the United States Army, joining the Job Corps.[7]

Marime laws are the most potent force behind maintaining social control within the Gypsy community and preventing assimilation into the dominant culture. All non-Gypsies and everything they touch is, by definition, *marime*. These laws inhibit Gypsies from mixing with non-Gypsies in any significant way. For this reason Gypsies have traditionally camped on the outskirts of *gaje* towns to avoid contamination. When the Gypsies are forced to come into contact with the *gaje* for business purposes, they do everything they can to minimize bodily contact. All fortunetelling parlors have a special chair for the client which is covered with extra fabric to prevent contamination. Whenever possible, Gypsies resist using public bathrooms, buses, and restaurants. When they do eat in restaurants they often order food which can be eaten without utensils and request paper cups. Their philosophy is: the less one has to do with the *gaje,* the better.

PROTECTIVE COLORATION

Thus far this study has described and analyzed the truly Gypsy aspects of Gypsy religion. However, during the past twelve hundred years the Gypsies have acquired numerous beliefs, saints, and religious ornaments in order to make their religion appear more civilized to the *gaje.* This attempt to appease the *gaje* has backfired on the Gypsies, who are accused by every society in which they dwell of being insincere followers of various faiths.

Historically, Gypsies have lived in Catholic countries like Spain, Italy, Poland, and France, certain Catholic regions of Yugoslavia and Germany, and in Mexico and the countries of Central and South America. Not surprisingly, they will most frequently say, upon being asked, that they are Catholic. But during the Inquisition, they were killed for being anything but Catholic (Tipler 1968:64). Consequently, the Gypsies now try to appear as Catholic as possible. In fact, during my fieldwork I never encountered a Gypsy who claimed to be of any faith other than Roman Catholic. Superficially, Gypsies try to appear Catholic by adopting as much Catholic camouflage as possible. For example, it is common to see Gypsies wearing crosses and crucifixes. Fortunetelling parlors are decorated with crosses, statues of the Virgin Mary, Jesus, and St. Anne. A successful fortuneteller explained the importance of decorating a fortunetelling parlor with Catholic effects: "The first thing you gotta do is go down to Tiajuana and buy a lot of that plaster crap. For twenty dollars you can get a Mary, a Jesus, and a lot of other saints. The people trust you more when you got these things. It makes them think you are closer to God." I have observed hundreds of Gypsy fortunetelling parlors with Catholic statues and crosses, but I have never observed a cross or statue of any religious figure in Gypsy living quarters. This contrast between their business and personal space is striking.

Other scholars who have studied Gypsies have noticed their insincerity toward Catholicism. While studying Mexican Gypsies, Pickett (1966b:92–94) observed that the Gypsies attended church only on Christmas and Easter. During those visits, which never lasted longer than five minutes, the Gypsies never knelt, touched holy water, or uttered a prayer. Pickett described them as looking around the church with curiosity and then leaving as soon as possible.[8] Additionally, Gropper (1975:112) has mentioned that Gypsies are skeptical of Christianity and dislike priests and nuns because they are celibate and unnatural. I can corroborate the Gypsies' negative attitude towards the Catholic clergy. During one of my Romany vocabulary lessons with two Gypsy children at the Lincoln Heights Public Library in Los Angeles, the children decided to teach me all the Romany swear words while four nuns were selecting books nearby; when I told the children they should be more respectful to the nuns, they replied, "So what. Let them go to hell."

But the Gypsies have integrated some saints of other faiths into their religion. A popular celebration for the Kalderash Gypsies is St. George's Day, celebrated in April each year. The *Rom* adopted St. George, a Greek Orthodox saint, when they experienced good luck after spending a period of time in a cave in Byzantine Greece which had his image carved into the wall (Sampson 1923:168).

Borrowed from the Catholic Church is the famous pilgrimage of Saintes-Maries-de-la-Mer. Each year on May 24 and 25 the *Rom* of France, Italy, and Spain make a pilgrimage to the south of France to pay homage to Sara, the Black Virgin. According to the Catholic Church, Sara, the servant of the three Marys—Mary Salome, Mary Jacobe, and Mary Magdalene—is believed to have followed her mistresses to the south of France and landed at the village of Saintes-Maries-de-la-Mer (McDowell 1973:38–49). She was not canonized, but in 1448 King Rene the Good declared that loyal Catholics pay homage to this saint (Clébert 1967:179–83). For the Catholics, the yearly pilgrimage has become a blessing of Saint Sara and the sea. For the Gypsies, Saintes-Maries-de-la-Mer is a joyous occasion which affords them the opportunity to see old friends and relatives, make business contacts, arrange and celebrate marriages, and to adjudicate legal matters and hold *pomanas* (Clébert 1967:179–83; Lopez and Yoors 1974:122–23). The Gypsies pay respect to the wooden statue of Sara by touching or rubbing cloth garments which are placed on her for the celebration; they believe this rubbing brings good luck. The Gypsies may have been celebrating the festival of Saintes-Maries-de-la-Mer for as long as the French Catholics, but not in the same way.[9] Clearly, the Catholic religious significance of the pilgrimage has been shed by the *Rom* as they incorporated it into their own religion. Interestingly, North American Gypsies celebrate St. Anne's Day on July 26 in Quebec, Canada, at the Basilica of Saint-Anne-de-Beaupré in the same spirit as European Gypsies celebrate Saintes-Maries-de-la-Mer. Similarly Gypsies in Honduras make an annual pilgrimage to the Christ of Esquipulas in Southern Guatemala on January 14 (Max and Max 1969:7).

CONCLUSION

It would be a mistake to think that the Gypsies' religion can be traced to the holidays they celebrate. Gypsies are an extremely gregarious people who enjoy celebrating. For example, it is common practice for Gypsies in North America to celebrate Christmas and Easter twice a year—once according to the American calendar and again following the Greek Orthodox calendar. They have also adopted Thanksgiving and New Year's as religious holidays (Cohn 1973:33–35). In this chapter I examined the Gypsy religion and attempted to distinguish between the truly Gypsy elements and those incorporated from other religions for protective coloration or pleasure.

Reflecting a gross misunderstanding of the Gypsies' religious beliefs, Tompkins (1971:2) has dismissed the Gypsies' religion as "basically Christian with a lot of hocus pokus [sic] added." The Gypsies are not Christian and never have been, although they have successfully convinced outsiders that they are. In fact, the Gypsy religion is more similar to Judaism than to Christianity. Like Jews, the Gypsies are monotheistic, do not make graven images of their god, and do not accept Jesus Christ as their Savior or as the Son of God. They practice circumcision of their sons, adhere to strict anticruelty laws, observe family and communal purity laws (*marime*), and engage in numerology. Unlike Jews, the Gypsies have an unshakeable belief in ghosts; they are not literate and, therefore, do not study the Five Books of Moses, the Mishnah, the Talmud, or any other body of Jewish knowledge.

Essential to the Gypsies' survival as an ethnic group is their fierce determination not to assimilate into the dominant society. Much of this determination stems from the Gypsies' belief that non-Gypsies are *marime*. The *marime* codes keep the physical and social contact between the Gypsies and outsiders to a minimum. Such solidarity within the Gypsy community is fortified by anticruelty laws and belief in ghosts. Violence and excessive abuse are not tolerated within the Gypsy community, and Gypsies are expected to treat one another humanely or be excommunicated from the group. From the Gypsies' point of view, life within the Gypsy community is safe and secure, while life outside the community is reckless and even dangerous. Thus, the Gypsies' position as middlemen is enhanced by their religious beliefs, which lead them to see the outside world as symbolically impure and fraught with hazard.

Chapter 5

THE GYPSY FAMILY

STRONG ADHERENCE to Gypsy religious beliefs is ensured by the Gypsy family and tribal structure. Gypsies, like other middleman groups, have cultivated an elaborate kinship structure which enables them to resist assimilation into the dominant society and succeed economically. In this chapter I examine Gypsy family and kinship structure, including Gypsy patterns of courtship, marriage, divorce, and child custody. I also discuss Gypsy attitudes toward various phases in the life cycle, including childhood, adolescence, adulthood, and old age.

Each Gypsy has four loyalties and identities: his or her nation, *kumpania, vitsa,* and extended family. In the world Gypsy community there are at least thirteen Gypsy nations; every Gypsy is a member of one of these nations. *Kumpanias* are groups of extended families, often but not always of the same nation, who occupy a particular geographic territory. The *kumpania* is the social, political, and economic unit which maintains and enforces the rules of Gypsy life. Each *kumpania* agrees upon a leader who will represent the group in dealings with other Gypsy *kumpanias* and with outsiders, such as welfare workers, city attorneys, the police, and other persons of *gaje* authority. This leader is known as "the chief" to the *gaje* and the *Rom baro* (big man) to the Gypsies.

The erroneous notion of the "king of the Gypsies" is based upon the "chief." In reality there is no "king" or "queen" of the Gypsies. The chief is the most respected member of the *kumpania*, owing to a flawless record of moral character, financial success, sound judgment, and the ability to deal with the *gaje* on their turf. Despite the extremely high illiteracy rate for Gypsies, chiefs usually can read and write to some extent. The chief has authority in matters of business and migrations and presides over the *kris* (Clébert 1967: 162–63).

The female counterpart of the chief is the *phuri dae* (old mother), often the wife of the chief, but not always. Technically, the power of the *phuri dae* is restricted to matters of women and children, but since the Gypsy women are an important financial force within the *kumpania*, the *phuri dae* is consulted in all matters (Clébert 1967:194; Rao 1975:144). I know of several California *kumpanias* headed by women.

The *kumpania* is composed of a loose federation of extended family groups called *vitsas*. It is difficult to know how many *vitsas* a particular chief controls, but the average is about one hundred (Clébert 1967:163). Several families, usually headed by siblings or first cousins, unite to form a *vitsa. Vitsas* function as huge extended families which work together as an economic unit.

Ever since the study of Gypsies started, scholars have debated whether the *Rom* are matrilineal or patrilineal. Clébert (1967:165–66) insists that Gypsies are matrilineal, while Gropper (1975:76–77) has demonstrated that the Gypsies she observed in New York City are patrilineal. I have found American Gypsies to be mainly patrilineal. The confusion about how the Gypsies trace their lineage is created by non-Gypsy social scientists who have tried to comprehend Gypsy kinship by using preconceived categories. However, the Gypsies are an extremely practical people; to them kinship means identification with the side of the family that offers the best financial opportunity (Brown 1929:169; Okely 1975:78–81; San Roman 1975:180). Adams et al. (1975:80–81) have assigned the Gypsies' practicality the anthropological term "cognatic," which suggests that Gypsies claim either the mother's or the father's kin.

The Economic Basis of Gypsy Kinship

Gypsies practice economic territoriality by dividing every town, city, region, state, and country into units of economic potential. The Gypsy map of the United States is very different from the map used by non-Gypsies. Various Gypsy *kumpanias* control not only cities but also major arteries and intersections of all roads and highways. To those unaware of the Gypsy economy, what appears to be a random fortunetelling parlor is in reality a carefully negotiated territory.

Once territories have been staked out by various *kumpanias*, there is very little room for expansion except through contracting marriages with other *kumpanias*. A smart marriage can consolidate the wealth, power, and authority of two *kumpanias* (Okely 1975:81; Sutherland 1975b:217). Conversely, to marry for love as the *gaje* do is viewed by the Gypsies as irrational behavior. Marriages, like territories, are carefully arranged for the betterment of the entire *kumpania* (Okely 1975:81–82).

"Sewing Up" California

A prime example of consolidation through marriage occurred on 1 August 1976, when Ranko Toma, nephew of Spiro Toma, the chief of the Southern California Machwaya *kumpania,* married Sima Lazlo of San Francisco. Sima is the granddaughter of *phuri dae* Persa Lazlo who has controlled San Francisco fortunetelling for over thirty years. This union in fact created the most powerful and wealthy alliance of Machwaya Gypsies in the western United States. This union, in cooperation with the smaller Machwaya *kumpanias* in Santa Barbara and Monterey, "sewed up" the most desirable territories in California for the Machwaya Gypsies and established an empire which will last for decades. This marriage has paved the way for cordial relations between these two formerly competitive groups and has led to more marriages and profitable business deals.

The Toma-Lazlo wedding, held at a large hotel in Inglewood, California, was attended by one thousand guests of both *kumpanias* and a small predictable group of *gaje* invited by Spiro Toma for public relations purposes. I was among the *gaje* guests as well as a judge, his wife, and a deputy city attorney. Spiro Toma himself remarked to me: "We finally corralled a Lazlo. There hasn't been a marriage between the Tomas and Lazlos since I married my wife over forty years ago. We are very pleased about this arrangement." The guests were pleased too, since the union of Ranko and Sima expanded the social and economic mobility of everyone in attendance, except the *gaje.*

Despite the lavishness of the wedding reception—a four-course sit-down dinner, unlimited liquor, hours of dancing with two bands (one playing popular "rock 'n roll," the other playing traditional Gypsy music)—the mood of the Gypsy guests can best be described as satisfied rather than joyous. There was a pervasive feeling in the hall that these people had just completed the negotiations of a long and difficult contract and were now looking forward to the benefits they might glean. This mood at Gypsy weddings appears to be universal. Adams, Okely, Morgan, and Smith (1975) report a similar tone at the weddings of English Gypsies: "It is clear that the gifts and costly celebration mark approval by parents and kin and also serve to impress rivals and allies with whom a new link may now have been created. . . . The wedding gatherings attended during field-work were not an indiscriminate get together for local Travellers [Gypsies] regardless of kin connections, but a meeting of interested kin groups and factions" (Adams et al. 1975:66).

The Toma-Lazlo union reflects an ideal type in Gypsy marriage. Obviously not all Gypsies have the same wealth and power as these two *kumpanias*. However, the Toma-Lazlo example is a good one to discuss because other less successful Gypsy *kumpanias* use it as a standard to emulate. Because marriage forms group alliances (Okely 1975:81), it is one of the best ways to increase or decrease political, economic, and social status among Gypsies. Given the practical motivations of the Gypsy point of view, romantic love and physical attraction are ridiculous reasons for marriage (Gropper 1975:8; Kephart 1982:38; Rehfisch 1975:101). Individual desires have no legitimacy and are always abandoned for what is best for the group.

Courtship

Dating or any pairing of single Gypsies is prohibited. According to traditional Gypsy wisdom, only "big trouble" results from allowing young people to date. Trouble is defined as premarital sex, which will reduce the girl's bride price at the time of marriage (Rehfisch 1975:106). When a girl or boy begins to show interest in a member of the opposite sex, efforts are made by the family to marry them off before they get into trouble (San Roman 1975:183). This does not mean that single Gypsies do not see members of the opposite sex; in fact, there is considerable exposure at social gatherings, allowing single people the opportunity to superficially socialize and learn who is available for marriage.

This form of social exposure begins quite early, especially for girls. From the onset of puberty, every Gypsy girl is expected to look and act her best at social functions, including *pomanas*. A thirteen-year-old Kalderash girl described the subtle husband-hunting that goes on from a very early age: "I know it probably sounds crazy to someone who isn't a Gypsy, but we all get dressed up to go to *pomanas*. I always say, 'Oh, boy! I'm going to a *pomana.*' It's exciting because everyone you know is going to be there. I have to wear my best clothes because I have to look like I would make a pretty *bori* [bride]."

American Gypsies are curious about the *gaje* dating process since they are exposed to it through television and the movies. Dating is a tempting but unfulfilled fantasy. Alepa Yordanko, a twenty-one-year-old Kalderash Gypsy, explained her situation regarding dating: "I can't go out on dates. My grandfather and the other Gypsies would kill me. There are a few guys I always talk to at weddings that are really cute. Sometimes they call me up and we talk about where we would go on a date. Then usually someone walks into the room and I have to hang up the phone. We always talk about sneaking out and meeting secretly, but it's just talk. I'm afraid to do it, and so are they."

After years of exposure to possible marriage partners, serious negotiations for marriage begin in the late teenage years. It is significant that during the past twenty years I have observed a rapid rise in the age the Gypsies consider appropriate for marriage. For example, in 1964 I attended a Kalderash wedding of a fourteen-year-old girl to a seventeen-year-old boy. At that time the ages of the couple were normative in the Los Angeles Gypsy community. Since 1964 the suitable age for marriage among Gypsies in the Unites States has pushed upward to approximately seventeen to twenty-one years of age for girls and eighteen to twenty-two years of age for boys. The practice of precocious marriage is becoming extinct among Gypsies in the United States and western Europe. A group of Gypsies in England surveyed by Adams, Okely, Morgan, and Smith (1975:56–57) reported that 53 percent of the women and 94 percent of the men were married at eighteen years of age or older. Similarly, Takman (1976:38) and Gustafsson (1973:29–30) have documented the rise in the normative age of marriage among Swedish Gypsies. San Roman (1975) has found similar trends in the age of marriage among Spanish Gypsies.

Traditionally, marriage negotiations are initiated by the boy's family (Gropper 1975:44–47; Pickett 1966b:97–98). However, nobody is caught by surprise when a representative of the boy's family approaches the chosen girl's family with an offer of matrimony. By the time negotiations begin, both extended families have already under-taken careful research. Each family "tests the water" by suggesting a match at various social functions, usually in the form of banter. No one jokes about a possible marriage unless it is seriously being considered.

Meticulous investigations are conducted by the future bride's and groom's families to determine the economic, social, and political soundness of the other family. The families determine economic success by asking these questions: (1) how lucrative is the mother's fortunetelling operation; (2) how much supplemental income is gen-erated through welfare benefits; (3) how successful are the father and other men of the *kumpania* in business endeavors such as roofing, body and fender work, blacktopping driveways; and (4) in the case of the Machwaya, what are the real estate holdings of the family.

The second consideration is the social status of the family. Pivotal in determining the family's social acceptability is whether or not any member of the extended family or the *kumpania* has ever been tried or sentenced for a *marime* offense. If the family has a good record, secondary considerations are given to other social responsi-bilities. For example, if the male members of the *kumpania* serve on the *kris*, do the members in attendance respect and follow their opinions or merely listen to their suggestions out of politeness? Whether or not a family has been tried and convicted of a *marime* offense reveals to a curious family how well the family members treat each other and how they conduct themselves within the larger group. Since family problems—wife-beating, child abuse, and adul-tery—are exposed and adjudicated at a *kris*, a family's moral behav-ior becomes a matter of public record. There are no secrets in the Gypsy community.

Economic success coupled with social status equals political power in the Gypsy community. Economic success alone is not enough. If a *kumpania* gets ahead financially by taking advantage of the *gaje*, that is one thing, but dishonesty or cheating among other Gypsies results in a permanent blemish for the offender and his or her entire *kumpania*. Political power is enjoyed by those Gypsies who have made money while living by the guidelines of *romania*. In the marriage market, a family will possibly contract a marriage with a less wealthy family but seldom with a family of lower social stand-ing. Using ritual purity as a measurement, there is a high degree of intramarriage between families of like social status.

Bride Prices

Once the families involved have thoroughly investigated one another and have computed all of the essential information, a formal offer of marriage is made by an agent of the boy's family to the girl's family (Sutherland 1975b:218). The sum of money involved in the *daro* (bride price) depends upon the wealth of the boy's *kumpania*. The large amounts of money seem fantastic to the *gaje*, but to the *Rom* they represent wise, practical investments in the future. Current bride prices in the United States range from $5,000 to $30,000, and it is rumored that Ranko Toma's family paid $30,000 for Sima Lazlo.[1] Since the Machwaya are the richest Gypsies in the United States, their bride prices fall at the high end of the scale, while bride prices for the poorer Kalderash *kumpanias* hover at the lowest end. I asked some Kalderash men if it were possible to buy a bride for less than $5,000. A marriageable young man answered me: "Don't you know that inflation affects the Gypsies too? For less than $5,000, you get a dog."

Gypsy families spend a lifetime saving for brides. Purchasing a fine *bori* is the responsibility of the extended family. If a family is short of cash, every member works extra hard to make up the difference. Small children who have no other method of earning money will beg in public places and contribute their earnings to the bride price. Most Gypsies in the United States view begging as distasteful, but to raise money for a good *bori* it is considered acceptable. Purchasing a fine *bori* is not only a sound investment for the future, but it has also become a symbol of how well a family can work together to accomplish family honor. A forty-five-year-old Kalderash Gypsy woman summed up her pride in contributing to the bride prices of her adopted brothers' wives: "My father adopted me even though I was a sick baby. He said I would bring him good luck. I did, too. He had three sons, and naturally they all had to have *boris*. I didn't get married until I was twenty-five years old because I wanted to give all of my money to my father so he could buy nice *boris*. When I didn't have a good day telling fortunes, I went out into the street and begged."[2]

The economic, social, and political status of the families involved fairly well determine the bride price, but certain personal attributes of the bride enter into calculations for the exact amount paid. The personal criteria on which the bride price is based are virginity, ability and talent as a fortuneteller, physical beauty, general health, and emotional disposition. Occasionally some exotic feature like natural blonde hair or blue eyes may boost the value of the bride (Gropper 1975:152). Once a bride price is agreed upon, gossip informs the Gypsy community of the exact amount. If a high bride price is agreed upon, it is a demonstration of status for both families.

By this logic, a divorced woman will not receive as large a *daro*, owing to her lack of virginity the second time around. And in rare cases when a Gypsy girl is punished for acting "crazy," she is literally given away. For example, social worker Sharon Rainier told me about a case of a Kalderash girl who ran away from her home to join the Job Corps at age nineteen. When the family finally got her back after some months, her mother dragged her into the welfare office and demanded that Rainier make an appointment for her with a psychiatrist in order to "get her head fixed" so she would never do it again. Even though the girl was still a virgin and really did not break any *marime* codes, a *kris* was held to decide her fate for living among the *gaje*. In an interview with me, Rainier described the final episode of this big incident:

> It was such a big deal, no Gypsy in the county would try the case. They called in Miso Ivanovich from Monterey, because he was Machwaya and very powerful. They figured he would pass an impartial sentence. He showed up in a gold Cadillac wearing a big cowboy hat. His wife wore all the jewelry she owned. He heard the case and sentenced the girl and her family temporarily *marime*. When the sentence was up, the family literally gave her away to a Kuneshti family in San Francisco. She was used as an example.[3]

Although marriage negotiation among the Gypsies is all business, there is a small element of personal choice. A boy or a girl does not have to marry the first person suggested as a spouse. A future bride has the right to refuse a marriage offer; however, she does not have the right to refuse offers indefinitely, and by the third or fourth proposal she is pressured into accepting the offer (Gropper 1975:78; San Roman 1975:184). It is important to point out that marriage is the only alternative for Gypsies. Nobody has the option to remain single unless they have a physical or mental handicap making marriage unlikely.

Gypsy women are socialized to accept an adult life in which the roles of wife and fortuneteller are inseparable. As demonstrated by the case of the nineteen-year-old girl who joined the Job Corps, alternative careers and lifestyles are not options. Since fortunetelling has proved to be profitable for the *Rom* in the United States, it is considered the best and only occupation for American Gypsy women.

The Wedding

Gypsy weddings are always elaborate. The ostentatiousness of the celebration depends on the wealth of the families involved. Gypsy weddings usually last three or four days, and the responsibility and expense for making the wedding celebration rests with the groom's family (Gropper 1975:157; Pickett 1966b:97). The marriage ceremony itself varies from country to country. Since many Gypsies in the United States derive from eastern Europe, their ceremonies are similar to those performed at Gypsy weddings in the Balkans. In a common ceremony in the United States the bride is incorporated into the groom's family symbolically in the form of a dance, a Balkan *kolo.*

Legal or religious ceremonies and marriage licenses are ignored unless a couple needs them for welfare purposes.[4] I have never attended a Gypsy wedding where a member of the clergy was present, much less officiating at. I asked a Catholic priest from a parish near my family's store why he never attended the Gypsy weddings held at his parish hall. He told me, "They don't really seem to be interested in a religious ceremony. They just rent the hall from our office when they need it." Then I asked several Gypsy families who had rented the church hall in the past why they had selected it; they replied that it was cheaper than the commercial halls in the area.

After a large hall in a church or a hotel is rented for the wedding, guests are notified through the grapevine. Wedding invitations are not mailed to guests; instead, Gypsies rely on word of mouth and telephone calls to invite celebrants. It is not unusual for eight hundred guests of all ages to attend a reception. I have often observed playpens and portable cribs set up for babies and small children at weddings. Men and women celebrate separately during the marriage festivities. They do not eat or dance together but instead enjoy the occasion with members of their own sex. This separation of the sexes is upheld in the exact manner in which the orthodox Jews follow the concept of the *mechitzah* (Hebrew for barrier or "that which separates"). The entertainment, like at the Toma-Lazlo wedding, is usually provided by both a rock band and another band playing traditional Gypsy songs and American songs translated into Romany.

A strong motivation for having a big wedding is the money collected from guests so the couple will have a good financial start. Since it is the custom for the newly married couple to live with the groom's parents for the beginning years of marriage, household items are not desired gifts. Cash is the only appropriate gift at a Gypsy wedding, and it is collected in two ways. In the first way a male member of the groom's family auctions off scarves to the male guests who each offer a sum of money for the scarf; then the auctioneer announces the bidder's name and the amount he is offering.[5] If the other wedding guests think that the bidder can afford more, they will boo and hiss until he raises his offer. In the second method of collecting cash a member of the groom's family hollows out a loaf of French bread and asks male guests to stuff it with money.

The idea of taking a honeymoon is foreign to Gypsies. The routine of married life begins soon after the wedding celebration. According to tradition, once a woman is married, she must cover her hair with a *diklo*, a scarf that is knotted at the nape of the neck (see Brown 1929:169; Clébert 1967:215; Sutherland 1975b:227). Twenty-five years ago it was uncommon to see a married woman without a *diklo*, but this tradition seems to be losing ground among American Gypsy women in recent years. In fact, today it is quite common to see married women without *diklos*, although I have noticed that most still wear them when attending traditional communal gatherings, such as weddings or *pomanas*. Often the women have a *diklo* made to match the dress they are wearing.

After the wedding, it is the custom in the United States for a Gypsy bride to live with her husband's family until she becomes a mother herself (Sutherland 1975b:229). During the first few years of marriage, the *bori* is subservient to her mother-in-law and other members of her husband's family. She is expected to help with cooking and cleaning, but, more importantly, she is retrained in fortune-telling and must learn to use the techniques her mother-in-law prefers. It is extremely important that the *bori* and her mother-in-law establish a smooth and productive working relationship because after the wedding they become business partners in the strictest sense. This seemingly oppressive relationship between the *bori* and her in-laws strikes a balance when she becomes pregnant. In the case of late pregnancy or illness, the *bori* can expect her mother-in-law and other members of her husband's family to relieve her of her household and business responsibilities.

Gypsy Childhood and Child-Rearing Practices

Once a couple has a child, they can elect to establish their own residence. But even if they live separately from the husband's parents, they still function in an extended family arrangement which incorporates the husband's parents, their unmarried children, and the other married sons and their wives and offspring. The mother-in-law, called the *sackra* in Romany, is the senior business partner among all of her daughters-in-law.

Child-rearing is the responsibility of everyone in the family unit. When children are under two years of age, they are usually tended at home by the grandparents (or, in some cases, the great grandparents) and the older unmarried children. After two years of age, children are taken to the *ofisa*, where they can play in the neighborhood or stay behind the *ofisa* in the part of the rented store converted for living space. In many cases, Gypsies operate fortunetelling businesses out of their homes by using the front room as an *ofisa* and the rest of the house as living quarters (Gropper 1975:61; Gustafsson 1973:77–79).

Around the age of ten years, Gypsy children begin a type of professional socialization. This professional socialization, which is quite casual, resembles the old-fashioned apprenticeship. Boys spend the day with their fathers, grandfathers, older brothers, and other male members of the family, accompanying them on business ventures (Gustafsson 1973:89). Girls stay with the female members of the family in fortunetelling establishments and welfare offices (Rao 1975:154–56). Thus, by keeping older children with members of their own sex, the Gypsies accomplish two goals: children receive occupational training and learn to cultivate good business sense; and Gypsy children are surrounded constantly with role models who provide information about appropriate sex-typed behavior for Gypsy adulthood.

Public School Attendance

Within the past decade, there has been a revolutionary trend among Gypsies of all countries to send their children to public school. While Gypsy parents would like their children to learn how to read, write, and perform basic arithmetic, education is not the primary reason they send their children to school. In recent years, welfare workers have moved to tie welfare benefits to the children's attendance at public school (Gustafsson 1973:51–66; Tillhagen 1967:31–32). Children help the Gypsies make money for the family through welfare benefits, and, additionally, the public school is a free babysitter. This attitude persists only until the children are ten or eleven years old, when their parents permanently remove them from school.

Interestingly enough, Gustafsson (1973), who analyzed and reported the failure of the Gypsy School in Stockholm, called one subheading of her study, "It's no use telling children below the age of ten years, they don't understand anything till then" (pp. 79–81). Whether Swedish or American, the Gypsies find it safe to send children under ten to *gaje* schools because "everything they are taught is wasted on them anyway." Therefore, Gypsies do not perceive early education as a threat to their way of life.

When not forced to attend public school, Gypsy children are fairly free to spend their days exploring the world of the *gaje*. Since fortunetelling parlors are always located in places with a lot of foot traffic or automobile traffic, the children spend their time in commercial districts. They are permitted to spend their time as they like, as long as it is in the company of another Gypsy child, usually a sibling or a first cousin. This freedom can become lonely. Gypsy children I interviewed often complained that they have "no one to play with." They are discouraged and often prevented from forming friendships with *gaje* children they meet in school. Commercial areas do not have many children, and the few available are often considered too dangerous as playmates for Gypsy children. Since the Gypsy practice of economic territoriality spaces fortunetelling establishments to avoid competition, there are seldom any Gypsy children in the residential or commercial neighborhood to play with, unless they are siblings or first cousins (Gropper 1975:59; Gustafsson 1973:101). But the loneliness of childhood ends when the Gypsy child is old enough to spend his or her day with the adults, learning how to become a *rom* and a *romni* (married woman). At this point they forget childhood and strive to become bona fide members of the *kumpania* and *vitsa*.

Divorce and Child Custody Among the Gypsies

During the early years of marriage, divorce is fairly common among the Gypsies (Brown 1929:167–69; Gropper 1975:162). It is not considered a serious problem unless children are involved (San Roman 1975:184). Because there is little knowledge of the opposite sex and girls are removed from their families to live as *boris* with their husbands' families, there are often regrets. It is extremely common for Gypsies to marry twice before they settle down into permanent married life (Pickett 1966a:8; San Roman 1975:182). Once children arrive, marriages usually remain stable.

The main issue in a divorce centers around the bride price. For this reason all divorces must be handled legally through arbitration before the *kris* (Sutherland 1975b:236–37). If the bride and her family can successfully convince the judges that she was mistreated by her husband and his family, then her father is entitled to keep the full amount of the bride price and his daughter (Pickett 1966b:97). In cases where the boy's family can prove that the divorce is the fault of the *bori*, her father is asked to return a large percentage of the bride price (Sutherland 1975b:292–97). When fault cannot be determined, the bride's father is usually allowed to keep a percentage of the money to compensate for his daughter's loss of virginity, which will force him to accept a lower bride price the second time around (Brown 1929:166; Clébert 1967:216; Gropper 1975:81). After the divorce, Gypsy women return home to their parents and assume the roles they had before they were married. A divorced woman does not gain any new freedom such as the option to date men; instead, she must wait once again for a marriage offer. The divorced men, like the women, similarly resume the old life they had before they were married (Gropper 1975:90–92). Usually both women and men wait one year before giving marriage another try.

Child custody is a far more complicated matter than divorce. Most problems in child custody matters can be traced to the cognatic kinship structure of the Gypsy community; since lineage can be traced through the mother or the father, there are no exact rules to determine which parents should be allowed custody in the case of divorce. San Roman (1975:185) has reported one exception to this problem: she has found that Spanish Gypsies award custody of children to the father's family unless he has deserted them. It appears that Gypsies handle child custody matters on a case-by-case basis. There always seem to be hard feelings about child custody among the Gypsies I have interviewed. In this respect they do not seem much different from their *gaje* counterparts.

Growing Old

The idea of retirement is unfamiliar to the Gypsies; they remain economically productive until ill health prevents otherwise (Adams et al. 1975:138; Okely 1975:66–67). Because fortunetelling is the type of skill that improves with experience, Gypsy women reach the zenith of their careers late in life. Old age is revered among the *Rom.* Younger members of the extended family and *kumpania* defer to the older members on all matters and seek their advice (Okely 1975:80; Max and Max 1969:3–4). Old people are not segregated by their age; instead, they continue to function as integral parts of the extended family and *kumpania*. Grandparents are actively involved in the rearing of children. The Gypsies do not need old age homes for their parents and grandparents because the children, grandchildren, and other members of the extended family and *kumpania* take care of the personal and financial needs of old people.

CONCLUSION

The Gypsy family structure is essential for the group's survival. Family relationships go beyond our expectations of the nuclear family. Because Gypsy families are the first line of defense against assimilation, children are both socialized to remain apart from the dominant society and simultaneously taught how to survive in it. Extended families not only provide nurturing and emotional support, but they also function as primary economic units. The extended family is a small business which works in cooperation with other families that are also small businesses. The economic aspect of family life governs marriages and the resulting kinship and geographical associations.

Without their family and kinship structure, the Gypsies could not function as a middleman minority. The cooperation of the extended family allows middleman minorities to avoid wage-labor jobs which would make them economically dependent on members of the dominant society and eventually force them to assimilate. Family cooperation in the form of loyalty, the pooling of financial and personal resources, and the willingness to work long hours leads to economic self-sufficiency and is a buffer against the pressures of assimilation.

Chapter 6

THE GYPSY LEGAL
SYSTEM AND PRACTICE
OF ECONOMIC
TERRITORIALITY

*T*HE SOCIAL and economic organization of the Gypsy community is regulated by the Gypsy legal system which enforces the traditional Gypsy law known as *romania*. Literally translated, *romania* means "the way of the *Rom*" (Sutherland 1975b:319; Tillhagen 1959a:18–31). To outsiders the Gypsies appear to be a lawless people who circumvent non-Gypsy law whenever possible. In reality, Gypsies are governed by the strict dictates and practices of *romania*, which is preserved and adjudicated by the most respected members of the community (Gropper 1975:97; San Roman 1975:188–94; Wedeck 1973:271). Since Romany is an unwritten language, there is no codification of the Gypsy laws; instead, an oral tradition is handed down from generation to generation (Gropper 1975:84–85).

In this chapter I will investigate two interesting dimensions of the Gypsy legal system: first, the role of the Gypsy court in establishing and maintaining economic territoriality; second, the way in which Gypsies administer justice to deviant members of their group by manipulating non-Gypsy authorities into carrying out their verdicts.

THE *KRIS*

Infractions of Gypsy law are heard by a Gypsy tribunal called a *kris* (pronounced "crease"), a judicial body of two to five adult males (Brown 1929:162–63; Tillhagen 1959a:19; Yoors 1967:172–74). Members of the *kris* are selected on the basis of their reputation as law-abiding Gypsies and their financial wealth.[1] In matters of serious importance or in cases where insiders cannot reach a solution, a member from another *kumpania* will be asked to serve on a *kris*. I cited an example of this practice in chapter 5 in the case of the nineteen-year-old girl who joined the Job Corps. In similar cases a lower-status *kumpania* will ask for the assistance of a higher status *kumpania* in reaching a judgment. There are no examples of the reverse situation occurring.

Evidence is presented by all disputing parties at the *kris* while adults from concerned *vitsas* or *kumpanias* listen. Verdicts, decided by the judges, are announced to the entire assembly. As a general rule, verdicts are accepted by the litigants and reinforced by all those present. Much of the success of the Gypsy legal system is because its judgments are public. Gossip and other methods of social control are utilized to carry out the intent of the law (San Roman 1975:192; Sutherland 1975b:100). For example, if the *kris* rules that a person and his or her family should be regarded as *marime* for a period of six months, the message is clear not only to the guilty party but also to all those assembled. *Romania* dictates that if anyone in the community conducts business, travels, or even shares a meal with the convicted party, they too will become *marime*.

Respect for *romania* and strict social control are usually enough to enforce the Gypsy way; however, there are individuals or family groups who defy the verdicts set down by the *kris* and live and work outside the pale of Gypsy law. Empirically, these renegade cases are the most interesting to the sociologist because they demonstrate the way in which Gypsies creatively manipulate the host society into enforcing their rules.

Kris *Procedures*

When Gypsies cannot settle a dispute informally in a *diwanya* (discussion among male members of the family tribe), a *kris* is called (Pickett 1966b:86).[2] Calling a *kris* is no small matter because it is financially costly and the results become a matter of public record. As in the case of a funeral, all Gypsies related to the involved parties are obligated by Gypsy law to attend the *kris*. For this reason it is necessary to announce the time and place of a *kris* at least four days ahead of time so everyone can be notified in enough time to make arrangements to attend. A *kris* is an urgent matter, and there is no excuse for not attending. If a *Rom baro* ("big man") is ill and cannot attend for health reasons, the *kris* is either postponed or held close to his home so he may attend.

In the United States it is the custom for the guilty party to pay for the *kris*, which involves renting a hall and supplying it with enough food and liquor for all those in attendance (Gropper 1975:96). In Sweden it is the custom for the person demanding the *kris* to pay for the travel expenses of all those who attend; even though the Gypsy population in Sweden is quite small compared to the United States, this practice can be extremely costly (Tillhagen 1959a:20–24). Making the *kris* a costly venture is an intentional practice to discourage unnecessary litigation.

The judges sit facing the witnesses, who present their side of the story without the use of an attorney. The plaintiffs and the defendants can bring as many witnesses as they wish, and evidence is commonly submitted to the *kris*. If those in attendance feel that a witness is lying or taking too long to answer the judges' questions, they will hiss and make jokes until the witness sums up his or her case.

The Gypsy system of justice is highly involved, going beyond cases we commonly refer to as criminal and civil lawsuits. The *marime* cases are tried with the intention of preserving the Gypsy way of life. If an individual Gypsy becomes too familiar with the *gaje,* it is perceived as a crime against the entire Gypsy people and tried before a *kris* to teach the transgressor a lesson and make an example of him or her (Gropper 1975:106–7; Sutherland 1975b:263; Tillhagen 1959a:12–21). This is the strongest method the *Rom* have of maintaining social control and strictly delineating insider-outsider boundaries (Yoors 1947:14–15).

Criminal cases include murder, assault, wife- and child-beating, rape, incest, adultery, unethical business practices which harm another Gypsy, and giving to the *gaje* any information harmful to other Gypsies. There is dual punishment for any of these criminal acts: one remedy is to financially compensate the injured party; the *marime* remedy excommunicates the guilty party and his or her entire *kumpania* either temporarily or permanently. The *marime* verdict is the most dreaded of the two, for the "veil of shame" hangs over the convicted party and his or her family for generations.

San Roman discusses a fine example of a criminal case tried by the *kris* (1975:192). In a Spanish Gypsy ward a young boy was throwing stones, and in the process he inflicted a serious head injury upon another Gypsy child. A *kris* was called, and it decided that the parents of the boy who threw the stone should pay the hospital bills and all other expenses related to the accident. In addition to this decision, the guilty boy's family was banished from the ward. Two years later when a relative of the family tried to move back into the ward, he was told that he was forbidden to live and work there. Financial compensation was only one part of the punishment; the larger part was the shame and disgrace of the *marime* verdict for the entire family.

From my fieldwork I can document three cases tried strictly as *marime* cases in which nobody was actually harmed, but the Gypsies involved violated the strict insider-outsider boundaries established by their ethnic group. The first case involved a low-status Kalderash male in his early twenties who joined the United States Army and was stationed in Germany. The *kris* for this young man was held in 1963. He did not attend because he was in Germany, but his brother and other family members were tried instead. He was sentenced permanently *marime*. When he returned from his tour of duty, he could not find a Gypsy bride, and other Gypsies would not conduct business with him. Six years later, when his niece became of marriageable age, her family had to travel to Chicago to find her a husband. The fellow she married came from a family who had also been sentenced as *marime* some time in the past. Within one year the girl was back home with her parents in California after her husband had severely beaten her. Her family's attitude to the "bad luck" was that they were "finished as Gypsies" ever since the father's brother joined the Army. To test the status of this excommunication, in conversation I mentioned the name of this family to a Machwaya Gypsy man, who told me: "Stay away from those Gypsies. They are out." (When he said the word "out," he made a gesture like an umpire would make at a baseball game.)

Another *marime* case tried by the *kris* was that discussed in chapter 5 involving the nineteen-year-old Kalderash girl who ran away from home and joined the Job Corps. This case is of particular interest because it is the only time I was able to interview a *gajo* who had participated in a *kris* proceeding. The *gajo* was Sharon Rainier, a northern California social worker who specializes in Gypsy cases. Ms. Rainier's participation as a witness is virtually unique because the Gypsies regard *kris* proceedings as highly sensitive and off-limits to non-Gypsies (Gropper 1975:96–97; Yoors 1947:2–4).

Rainier corroborated the impressions of other ethnographers who have studied the Gypsies and observed *kris* proceedings (Gropper 1975:96–102; Tillhagen 1959a:18–31; Yoors 1947:16–18). The hall where the *kris* was held had been rented many times in the past by the local Gypsies for weddings, *pomanas,* and celebrations for honored guests. Food and liquor were served at the end of a day of proceedings. This *kris* lasted three days and attracted about 250 Gypsies. Because this case was regarded as such a "big incident," the local members of the *kris* called in a wealthy Machwaya chief from Monterey to hear the case as a lone judge. These Kalderash Gypsies felt that a wealthy and respected Machwaya with a flawless record would render a decision that was impartial and correct. Rainier reported that she was cross-examined carefully by the judge in the same way an American prosecution attorney would cross-examine a witness. The judge asked Rainier to describe in detail the experience: what the Job Corps was; where the girl slept while she was there; if boys and girls were allowed to sleep together at the facility; what type of clothing girls typically wore at Job Corps training sessions; and, finally, why she encouraged Gypsy youths to join the Job Corps in the first place. Rainier believed that the judge and the 250 jurors were convinced she was telling the truth. She said she was asked to testify only because the Job Corps is a *gaje* institution which no Gypsy could describe in accurate detail.[3]

After three days of hearings, the judge rendered a verdict of temporarily *marime,* even though the girl was still a virgin and promised to return wholeheartedly to the Gypsy way of life. The decision was such a scandal that the girl's entire *vitsa* moved to San Francisco, where they lived as "untouchables" and had a great deal of difficulty making a living. Eventually the shamed girl was given away in marriage without a bride price to a Kuneshti boy.[4] Twelve years later, the girl's family was gradually seen again at Gypsy functions in the area. They have been given a few odd jobs to do by other Gypsies, but they will never be fully accepted again.

A third *marime* case involved a Kalderash woman who was sentenced for having a *baro muy* (big mouth). The woman, a San Francisco fortuneteller, allowed herself to be befriended by a freelance photojournalist, who promised her that she could arrange special training for the Gypsy woman's deaf child. Since the Gypsies have no folk methods for dealing with deafness, the mother felt desperate and leaped at the opportunity to have diagnostic testing and speech therapy for her child. Because the Gypsy mother trusted the journalist, she willingly answered questions about the Gypsy way of life and allowed herself to be photographed. The photojournalist, completely ignorant of Gypsy ways and the degree to which Gypsies safeguard anonymity, told some other Gypsies what this woman had told her. To make matters worse, the journalist published an article in a "cheap" magazine with pictures of the Gypsy mother and child.

The Gypsy communities of northern and southern California were outraged by this betrayal and called a *kris* to decide the woman's fate. A large crowd attended this *kris*. It was determined by the *kris* that the woman should have her fortunetelling territory taken away from her and be sentenced as *marime* for one year. A pathetic postscript to this case is that after the diagnostic testing and several therapy sessions, the center providing the services to the child lost its funding and closed, leaving mother and child once again without assistance and training.

Thus, one major function of the *kris* is social control over the Gypsy community. Consorting with the *gaje* for reasons other than business or extracting a needed service like medical or dental care is viewed as unlawful by the Gypsies. To endanger the security of other Gypsies by going out of the web is a "crime." *Marime* sentences are especially severe even by the Gypsies' admission, but they serve a viable function in maintaining boundaries between the Gypsies and the *gaje*.

As observed in chapter 2, Gypsies adhere to a philosophy similar to the orthodox Jewish concept of "building a hedge around the Torah." Orthodox Jews, according to this concept, construct a series of concentric rules to encircle and protect fundamental precepts. When one of the lesser rules is broken, it is treated as a partial violation of the larger precept. Owing to this practice, the most important precepts are seldom violated. Gypsies, like the Jews, have developed a series of lesser laws designed to protect major precepts like *marime* codes.

Given the severity of *marime* sentences, it would be unrealistic to assume that antagonism and outright conflict do not occur as a result of the Gypsy law. In general, Gypsies support the law and its administration with a high degree of cooperation; occasionally, however, Gypsies sentenced *marime* become renegades who, no longer concerned with the welfare of the group, strike out for themselves. Since these renegades have been excommunicated by the group, they are almost beyond Gypsy control and can create serious problems for the ethnic group. Gypsies typically deal with these renegades by appealing to the *gaje* authorities and using them to do their dirty work for them.

DEALING WITH RENEGADES

Thus, while the concept and administration of *romania* are respected to a high degree, deviance does occur. In most circumstances, deviants are Gypsies (and members of their families) who have been sentenced *marime*. Sometimes these deviants become renegades who live and work outside the bounds of *romania*. These renegades pose serious problems for the Gypsy community, often breaking *gaje* laws and creating a bad name for the entire ethnic group. The Gypsy community, having excommunicated these members, is practically powerless in exerting social control over them. Historically, the *Rom* have developed an ingenious method for dealing with these renegades: when they cannot control their coethnics, they appeal to the *gaje* to punish them (San Roman 1975:190–91; Sutherland 1975b:111–16; Tyrnauer 1977:59–63).

Relationships with Non-Gypsies

As observed in chapter 4, Gypsies limit their interactions with non-Gypsies to transacting business and procuring special services unobtainable within the Gypsy community. In addition to these types of interactions, the Gypsies cultivate contacts with non-Gypsies in positions of authority, such as state senators, assemblymen, mayors, city attorneys, police chiefs, and welfare workers. The Gypsies' major motivation for cultivating these contacts of authority is to help them maintain their own system of justice and ethnic boundaries. Gypsies use these *gaje* authority figures as a legal "strong arm" to discipline renegade Gypsies beyond their control. For the Gypsies to cultivate and maintain a working relationship with non-Gypsy members of authority, they must invest considerable time, effort, and money. Gypsy chiefs function as leaders of small "nations" and use diplomatic skills in these relationships.

Within the Gypsy community it is considered appropriate for only the chief and his sons or specially selected individuals to develop this sort of a relationship with the *gaje* (San Roman 1975:190; Sutherland 1975b:105–15). The chief and/or his sons have the delicate and awesome responsibility of developing a one-sided relationship with the *gaje*, in which they expose very little about their ethnic group while they simultaneously try to extract as much information as possible about the interworkings of the *gaje* political structure. Gypsy chiefs employ various methods of ingratiating themselves with non-Gypsy officials. In the beginning, the most common method for getting on the good side of the *gaje* is to invite them to a wedding or a saint-day celebration. During these celebrations, the chiefs will publicly flatter the honored guest with testimonials and tributes. Once a social relationship has been established between a particular Gypsy chief and a *gajo* official, the chief will continue to extend social invitations on a steady basis while at the same time demonstrating what a good citizen he is by making token gestures. For example, one Machwaya chief has been a member of a southern California city's volunteer fire department for twenty years. He never fails to invite the city attorney, mayor, or local judges to weddings or other celebrations regarded as safe in terms of inviting the *gaje*, and each summer this chief invites the city attorney and his family to spend a weekend on his ranch in Monterey, where the children can ride horses.[5]

Another example is the chief of the Kalderash Gypsies in central California, who has been successful in charming various minor politicians, bureaucrats, and major state figures. In fact, he met with both Ronald Reagan and Jerry Brown when they were California governors. This chief, George Anders, showed me photographs of himself with each former governor, proudly displayed in his living room.

The most remarkable example of a Gypsy chief who has nurtured *gaje* political contacts is Joey Maxwell, a Seattle used car dealer. Through years of effort, Maxwell has built a political pipeline that extends from local governmental agencies all the way to the federal level. After cultivating a relationship with a United States senator, Maxwell forged ahead and learned enough about the *gaje* structure to push several programs that benefited his coethnics while consolidating his power within his own ethnic group. In 1968, Maxwell observed Hispanic, black, American Indian, and Asian leaders vying for special assistance and funding to help their groups integrate into American society. Maxwell seized this opportunity to make special gains for the Gypsies and himself by flying to Washington, D.C., to meet with officials of the Department of Health, Education, and Welfare.[6] The result of Maxwell's diplomacy was HEW's official acknowledgment that the Gypsies were a bona fide minority group in the United States, thereby making them eligible for funding privileges.

With this funding, Maxwell established a Head Start program for Gypsy children, which operated out of his storefront home, and a Division of Vocational Rehabilitation program on his used car lot. The DVR program taught the Gypsy men reading and basic accounting skills in addition to their on-the-job training. The official goal of the DVR program was to help Gypsy men pass the written test required to obtain a license to buy and sell used cars, since this is the common occupation for Gypsy men in the state of Washington and the rest of the United States (Tyrnauer 1977:30–32). However, these projects failed to endure when Maxwell could not conduct them on his own personal turf. When HEW or DVR officials wanted to change project sites or bring non-Gypsies into the programs, they were met with total resistance from Maxwell. The bureaucrats accused the chief of trying to reap tax benefits and other economic gains by insisting the projects be located on his property (Tyrnauer 1977:39–41).

What distinguished Maxwell from other ethnic leaders was his motivation to wield more power among Gypsies in the western United States, particularly among those Gypsies no longer controlled by the *kris*, rather than promote assimilation among his coethnics. Local, state, and federal funding provided additional revenue, but, more importantly, these programs granted Maxwell tighter control over the social, political, and economic activities in his territory. The Gypsies did not need a DVR school to learn how to be successful in the used car business. Instead, the DVR school gave Maxwell ultimate control in determining which Gypsies sold cars in the state of Washington. By knowing the laws and those who enforced them, Maxwell obtained the connections to legally prevent any Gypsy from doing business in his territory. This was a simple task since only the Gypsies that Maxwell approved could attend his school and learn the skills needed to obtain a license; all other Gypsies in the used car business were operating without a license and thus working illegally. These privileges empowered Maxwell to handle renegades otherwise out of his control (Tyrnauer 1977: 59–60).

Maxwell illustrates how Gypsy chiefs manipulate the non-Gypsy social structure to support their internal politics. This excerpt from the Washington DVR files demonstrates how commonplace this type of behavior is:

> In another Washington city, an official recommended to his superior in Olympia that a proposed project not be initiated because of factional disputes within the Gypsy community. He described a 2½ hour meeting in his office with fifteen members of the Gypsy community as "total chaos." He was taken aback by their style of debate and felt that they were less interested in the "rehabilitative" benefits of the particular project than in the opportunity it afforded them for "exploitation of the state of Washington" (Tyrnauer 1977:46).

It is common for non-Gypsies dealing with Gypsy chiefs to describe them as so opportunistic that they will turn one another in for the smallest offense. The factional disputes mentioned in the above excerpt probably arose over issues of territoriality, not merely dollars and cents. But since the Gypsy chiefs expose only a staged presentation to the *gaje,* they are misunderstood intentionally. The *Rom* would prefer the *gaje* to believe that they are fighting over money and petty jealousies than have them know the interworkings of Gypsy society. During the many interviews I have conducted with *gaje* authority figures, there emerged the recurring theme that "these people are so socially degenerate, even their own leaders would squeal on them in order to make an extra dollar."[7]

I have not encountered one *gaje* in any position of authority, minor or major, who realized that the peccadilloes that chiefs report to them have nothing at all to do with the actual offense they are trying to remedy. Many Gypsy chiefs have turned in fellow Gypsies for not paying parking tickets. The offense of not paying parking tickets is considered minor by everyone's standards, Gypsies and non-Gypsies alike. However, the motivation behind a chief's gesture like that one is to discipline a recalcitrant tribe member who is breaking the Gypsy law code either socially or economically. If the chief can succeed in getting the *gaje* officials to force this renegade into court and make him pay his tickets and a fine, then this chief has communicated to the renegade and all other members of his ethnic group that he has obtained power beyond the *kris* and traditional means of sanction.

Gypsy Authorities and Welfare Fraud

Welfare is another area where Gypsy chiefs will inform on wayward Gypsies as a form of social control. One Gypsy chief reported a couple for welfare fraud when he learned that they were collecting multiple benefits under assumed names. The couple, living in the chief's territory without permission and not belonging to his *kumpania*, was nevertheless trying to work and live in his territory "illegally." The situation was intolerable to the chief for several reasons. First, the couple never paid him a call of respect when they came to town; this obvious lack of Gypsy protocol was both a glaring insult to the chief and his followers and an act of open defiance. Second, the couple was indeed carelessly commiting welfare fraud. This behavior endangered their own financial security as well as the security of the entire *kumpania*.[8]

It became the responsibility of the chief to prevent this couple from disrupting the stability he and his followers enjoyed in that community. The chief, who knows the welfare code thoroughly despite his inability to read and write, makes certain that everyone in his *kumpania* is honest with the welfare department. Since this couple's behavior was so deviant it was unlikely they would respond to traditional authority, the chief had no choice but to report their misconduct to the welfare officials with the statement: "Please check out these Gypsies. I think they are cheating the welfare department, and it hurts me since you people have been so nice to us." The welfare department investigated the couple and found them to be in violation of the welfare rules. The couple was fined, and their welfare benefits were stopped. Shortly thereafter the couple left town. The chief, through Gypsy-style diplomacy, had restored the community's stability, averted a potential problem, and maintained his authority.

Maintaining Romania

Gypsy chiefs have the overwhelming responsibility of maintaining and enforcing the dictates of *romania*. When renegade members of the ethnic group strike out for themselves, they endanger the security of all Gypsies. Renegades (those people sentenced *marime*) have, as Gypsies, suffered the worst humiliation. They have been deprived of an honorable social and family life and forced to earn a living without the benefit of a secure territory. It is not surprising when these renegades express their anger and strike out at the community that has humiliated them. The best examples of this type of behavior resulted in a best-selling book, *The King of the Gypsies* (Maas 1975), later made into a movie of the same name.

Steve Tene, a New York-based Gypsy who descends from a family who has been sentenced *marime* many times, sold his version of "Gypsy life" to author Peter Maas for $50,000 (Rosenfield 1978:26–27). In his account of Gypsy life, Tene reinforced every negative Gypsy stereotype that non-Gypsies hold. Additionally, he embellished his story with exotic stories of sex, violence, and depravity. What Maas or his readers did not learn about Gypsy life was the truth. Tene later admitted that his story was not entirely accurate: "We do not curse our dead. I did not shoot my father. Gypsies are not all thieves. We do tell fortunes, but we do not all drive Cadillacs" (Rosenfield, 1978:27). But saying those things to Peter Maas made Tene a wealthy man, and he became wealthier when he received $180,000 for the film rights to the book (Rosenfield 1978: 26–27).

Every Gypsy chief in the United States and Canada was in a rage over what Tene had done. Many Gypsy communities tried to stop the production of the film through legal means, but none of the lawsuits proved successful. Gypsies like Tene are rare, but they do exist and cause problems for their ethnic group. It is the responsibility of Gypsy chiefs to deal with these renegades and curtail this type of behavior. While the chiefs cannot stop every renegade from causing trouble, to an amazing extent they have their coethnics under control through traditional legal means or diplomatic measures with the *gaje* authorities who unknowingly act as their "strong arm."

Economic Territoriality and the Kris

The most frequently adjudicated matter among the Gypsies is economic rights. According to *romania,* every Gypsy has the right to earn a living (Adams et al. 1975:114–16; Gropper 1975:98; San Roman 1975:187). Due to this basic philosophy, the Gypsies, both past and present, divide cities, counties, states, and entire countries into units of money-making potential. The *Rom* practice a strict form of economic territoriality.

The Gypsy map of any country is divided into urban and rural areas. Urban areas are subdivided into downtown and shopping districts. The only urban areas that interest Gypsies are those which attract heavy foot or automobile traffic. In high density cities like New York, fortunetelling locations are spaced every three blocks; in cases where Gypsies own the building in which they operate their business, they are granted a ten-block protective zone (Gropper 1975:98–99). Similar spacing laws exist in San Francisco and Chicago. In cities which are spread out like Los Angeles, Houston, Dallas, and Seattle, fortunetelling territories are divided up by major traffic intersections and main arteries.

Rural areas are divided into counties. For example, in Virginia there is one fortuneteller in each rural county. In Williamsburg, Virginia, the only town in James City County, there is one *kumpania;* the closest Gypsy fortuneteller is fifty miles away in the next county. But in rural California, due to the larger populations, fortunetellers are more closely spaced. In the case of Fresno, a city surrounded by agricultural lands, there are three fortunetelling establishments in the downtown area. The typical modus operandi for Gypsies in rural areas is to have one fortuneteller in town and the others strategically spaced along the highways.

The Gypsy map includes other types of economic territories like seafront wharves, vacation and recreational areas, amusement parks, carnival and circus sites. An informed observer will notice one fortunetelling parlor on every wharf along the east and west coasts of the United States and Canada. I have also observed seafront fortunetelling operations in England and Wales; in Brighton, England, two of the oldest English Gypsy families, the Boswells and Petalungros, have fortunetelling parlors on the wharf.[9] In the Welsh industrial cities of Cardiff and Swansea, there are Gypsy fortunetellers in the wharf areas. And in California, Gypsy fortunetellers have operated for years on the wharves of Santa Monica, Redondo Beach, Shell Beach, Monterey, and formerly the Long Beach Pike.

While the Gypsies' practice of economic territoriality is strict, it is not static. The Gypsy economy is a fluid and flexible one; its participants are continuously vying and negotiating for better and more territory. It is the responsibility of the *kris* to ensure each Gypsy's territorial rights while arbitrating over trades, mergers, and other forms of economic aggrandizement. The only way in which a Gypsy can increase his or her territory without the involvement of the *kris* is through a marriage alliance. Marriage is the most popular method of gaining and consolidating territory among Gypsies since it circumvents the potential problems of a *kris* and the limitations it might impose.

Problems occur when a *vitsa* violates the Gypsy map of a particular area. If the Gypsies who legally reside and work in an area catch another Gypsy working that territory, they have the right to call a *kris*. For first offenses, the *kris* usually issues encroachers a strong warning to desist in their unlawful behavior or risk a *marime* sentence and losing their own territory. The first hearing is designed to be a very humiliating experience. For example, when a Los Angeles Kalderash woman was discovered telling fortunes at a hot dog stand in someone else's territory, she was brought before the *kris*, publicly shamed, and then ordered to move her family's residence out of the territory. She was given three weeks to move. When after three weeks she could not find a place to live, she petitioned the *kris*, asking for an extension. At the extension hearing, witnesses who had functioned as spies for the *kris* during the three-week intervening period testified that the woman had kept her word and had ceased telling fortunes in the designated area. Owing to this good behavior, the woman was granted a generous extension to find suitable housing elsewhere, with a sworn promise that she would continue to obey the wishes of the *kris*.[10]

In the course of my fieldwork I have encountered numerous examples of the Gypsies' practice of economic territoriality. While studying the *Rom* of Virginia, I telephoned a Gypsy fortuneteller in

Newport News who advertised herself in the yellow pages as Sister Sapphire, a palmist and astrologist.[11] The following conversation ensued:

> A man answered the telephone. When I asked to speak to Sister Sapphire, he asked, "What's your name?"
> Sway: Marlene.
> Man: Have you ever been here before?
> Sway: No.
> Man: Well, then, how do you know about us?
> Sway: I saw your ad in the yellow pages, and I would like my palm read.
> Man: Hold on.
> In the background there was a lot of noise and confusion. People were speaking English and Romany. There was also a television blasting.
> Sister Sapphire: Yeah, who are you? What's your name?
> Sway: Marlene. I would like my fortune read.
> Sister Sapphire: Have you ever been here before?
> Sway: No.
> Sister Sapphire: Well, how did you find out about me? Friends of yours been here or something?
> Sway: No. I saw your ad in the yellow pages.
> Sister Sapphire: What are you, black or white?
> Sway: White.
> Sister Sapphire: What's your name?
> Sway: Marlene.
> Sister Sapphire: Where do you live?
> Sway: Williamsburg.
> Sister Sapphire: There's a fortuneteller in Williamsburg. Go to her.
> Sway: She isn't home.
> Sister Sapphire: Yes she is.
> Sway: No, I called her, and no one was there today.
> Sister Sapphire: What's the matter? Did she break her neck or something?
> Sway: I don't understand.
> Sister Sapphire: You go to her, honey. She's got a lot of girls there. Someone is always there. They don't leave the house alone. They got too many things in there.
> Sway: Won't you read my palm?
> Sister Sapphire: No, you go to her. She'll do it.

Then Sister Sapphire abruptly terminated the conversation by hanging up on me.

Later that week I obtained an interview with Madame Tina, the

Williamsburg fortuneteller, and her extended family. When I explained Sister Sapphire's unwillingness to tell my fortune, Madame Tina responded: "She's such a bitch. It looks like she is finally going to stop stealing my customers. We had to go to court, honey, to control that woman. She probably thought you were a spy or something. She's on good behavior this month." Then Tina's husband added: "She lives in Newport News, right on the highway. She gets all kinds of customers, even people from the navy base. Here we are stuck in Williamsburg next door to a farming supply store, big deal. We need all the customers in our area. She doesn't need one of ours." I asked Madame Tina if she were referring to the state court of Virginia or the Gypsy court when she mentioned having to take Sister Sapphire to court in order to control her. She explained that it was a local Gypsy *kris* who issued a warning to Sister Sapphire to mind her own territory.

Another example of the Rom's practice of economic territoriality was revealed during an interview I had with a man who owns property on a northern California wharf. The landlord said he owned a shop which had been continuously rented by Gypsies during the past fifteen years and used as a fortunetelling parlor. Recently the shop had remained vacant for several months. A different group of Gypsies, unfamiliar to the owner, inquired about renting the space. When the landlord said it would require a $3,000 deposit, a Gypsy man in the group handed the landlord $3,000 in cash, and they agreed upon the terms of the lease. The landlord mentioned that the Gypsies could not read the lease and asked him to explain it to them. Three days later the same Gypsy who gave the landlord the deposit asked for his money back. He explained that they were not local Gypsies, and many Gypsies were angry when they learned that the new Gypsies had intended to start a fortunetelling parlor at that location. The would-be tenant said he wanted to avoid trouble.[12]

Thus far in this chapter I have only discussed economic territoriality in terms of fortunetelling locations. Because fortunetelling is the most lucrative of all of the Gypsy occupations in the United States, Canada, and western Europe, territories are economically assessed by their ability to support a fortunetelling parlor, called an *ofisa*. In a typical middleman fashion, Gypsies usually live in the same building in which they operate their *ofisa*. In the case of the Monterey wharf property and other better locations, the Gypsies, not permitted to live in the *ofisa*, try to live as close as possible. In this way the location of the fortunetelling parlor is central; all other economic activities are secondary. However, these secondary activities, performed mostly by men, must be conducted within the boundaries of the fortunetelling territory. If the men of the *vitsa* appeal to the *kris* that the area is too small and does not yield a large enough profit, they can be granted more territory elsewhere. This second territory may or may not adjoin the first territory, and the types of activities performed in the second territory are strictly regulated. Under no circumstances can their wives, mothers, or daughters tell fortunes in the second territory, even on an occasional basis.

One economic activity of Gypsy men is the overseeing of the *ofisa*. It is the males' responsibility to provide protection for the *ofisa*, conduct all official business (paying deposits and rent), and promoting the fortunetelling business by passing out handbills (*bilyah*) advertising the operation. Other male Gypsy occupations include the buying, fixing up, and selling of used cars, trucks, and boats, body and fender work, blacktopping driveways, roofing, and, for the Machwaya, real estate investment. All of these activities must be conducted in the first or second territory. Buying real estate in another Gypsy's territory is absolutely forbidden.

Yugoslav Gypsies at the Tumacacori Mission

Vast as it is, the United States has very little worthwhile unmapped Gypsy territory. This was made abundantly clear in February of 1974 when a band of 102 Yugoslav Gypsies appeared in the Arizona desert. The group, illegally smuggled into the United States via Mexico, had been robbed and abandoned by their escorts in the desert near the old Mission Tumacacori, forty miles south of Tucson. The media followed the story for a while, depicting this band of Yugoslav Gypsies as a tribe of lost souls stranded in a desert wilderness.[13] But the American Gypsy community perceived this group differently: they created a disruption in the territorial equilibrium of the Gypsy economy. The biggest problem facing the American Gypsy community was how to successfully integrate this brethren group into their economy without hurting other Gypsies. To resolve the problem of the Yugoslav Gypsies, a monumental *kris* was held in Los Angeles to determine where to place the newcomers. It is estimated that over a thousand Gypsies attended from all over the United States, Mexico, and Canada. Every Gypsy *kumpania* sent a representative to the *kris* to make certain that their interests were protected. Finally, after two weeks of debating, it was decided by the *Rom baro* (big men) that the newcomers should take up residence and business activities in a run-down section of downtown Chicago. This decision was final, and in 1988 the Yugoslav Gypsies remain in that exact territory.

In addition to determining where to place these Yugoslav Gypsies, the *kris* had to address itself to the problems of their illegal status in the United States. The new group faced deportation hearings. Interestingly enough, it was easier for the *kris* to deal with the United States Immigration Office than with feuding members of its own ethnic group. In a characteristically clever move, the Gypsies avoided deportation by being "citizens of nowhere." The chief of the band, Ivan Konovalov, told an Immigration Services district director, "We are not citizens of any country, so we are not here illegally. There is no way we can be deported, because we have no country" (*Los Angeles Times* 1974a:17). Once the group settled in Chicago, the immigration authorities started deportation hearings against them. Although the Gypsies claimed they had neither passports nor money to travel, they asked to be deported to the Netherlands (*Los Angeles Times* 1974c:19). Official word from the Netherlands was that the Dutch authorities could not issue the Gypsies visas because they did not possess United States travel documents; meanwhile, the United States refused to issue the Gypsies travel documents because they were not citizens or refugees. Thus, the Gypsies, with the advice of the American coethnics, trapped the immigration bureaucrats in their own procedures. The result of the deportation hearing was best stated by Chicago Immigration and Naturalization District Director David Vandersall: "For all intents and purposes, they're here to stay" (*Los Angeles Times*, 1974b:38).

CONCLUSION

Living as self-contained nations within other countries, Gypsies handle their affairs with inventiveness. *Romania* is upheld by the *kris* which exercises ultimate authority over Gypsies. Decisions handed down by the *kris* are well enforced due to a high degree of solidarity in the Gypsy community. Since all legal action is made public, the Gypsies feel it is an honest system. Without their elaborate legal system and practice of economic territoriality, the Gypsies would not be able to survive in dominant societies.

In practicing economic territoriality, the Gypsies guarantee one another the right to earn a living free from the competition of a coethnic. If a Gypsy *kumpania* is industrious, thrifty, and aggressive, it will be successful. If a *kumpania* is lazy and does not build the potential of its territory, then it has no one to blame but itself. The system ensures an opportunity, but it does not ensure success. Gypsy *kumpanias* that take a bad territory, like the Yugoslav Gypsies in downtown Chicago, and make it lucrative are highly respected. This success has made them very desirable in terms of arranging marriages for their children and grandchildren.

Since the Gypsies do not use violence in solving their problems, they have had to invent another method for dealing with renegade members who have been excommunicated and act in ways which destabilize or endanger the community. To do this, the Gypsies cultivate ties with members of the dominant group who are in positions of authority. These *gaje* unknowingly help the *Rom baro* control and punish the renegades.

Chapter 7

ECONOMIC ADAPTABILITY

HE GYPSIES have survived culturally and economically for twelve hundred years in the Diaspora. Their cultural survival, discussed in preceding chapters, is tightly interwoven with their economic survival. To survive in a variety of hostile host settings, the Gypsies have developed a number of highly flexible and resilient business practices. Gypsies, like other middleman minorities, rely on family labor, intraethnic cooperation, a dual ethic, and a hard work ethos which give them the competitive edge over members of the host society. But Gypsies go beyond typical middleman behavior emerging as a middleman group par excellence. I will focus on this distinction of the Gypsies as an ideal type of a middleman minority in this chapter.

Unlike Jews, Chinese, Armenians, Indians, Japanese, and other middleman minorities, Gypsies are largely illiterate. As a consequence of their illiteracy, the educated and professional classes including attorneys, historians, sociologists, and politicians lack Gypsies who could represent their interests as an ethnic group on various levels. Yet despite this obvious liability, the Gypsies have managed to exploit one middleman niche after another and endure as a commercially successful ethnic group.

STRATEGIES OF ECONOMIC ADAPTATION

Ironically the central reason for Gypsy success has been the severe adversity with which they have had to contend throughout history. Adaptation to hostile circumstances has forced the Gypsies to develop a high degree of flexibility, which has resulted in at least five practices enabling them to endure: (1) nomadism; (2) exploitation of natural resources or resources viewed as worthless by society; (3) avoidance of sex-typing in the division of labor; (4) avoidance of age barriers in the distribution of labor; and (5) willingness to pursue more than one occupation.

The Gypsies have developed these five traits in more than forty different host societies. Owing to their relatively late arrival in Europe and North America, their deviant cultural attributes, illiteracy, and limited skills, the Gypsies have been forced into one precarious middleman niche after another. The Gypsy economic niches of fortuneteller, horse dealer, brickmaker, herbal medicine manufacturer, bear leader, and other exotic professions lack appeal for other segments in any particular society. While the niches Gypsies have occupied have been low-status, demeaning, and occasionally exotic, this does not prove that they have not established themselves as bona fide business people; it only suggests that they have exploited the most undesirable economic niches to their fullest potential.

The Gypsies' historical willingness to undertake work that no one else wanted has led them to develop the attitude that earning money even under the most humiliating circumstances is still honorable and productive. As a result of this attitude, the Gypsies, unlike other middleman groups, actively seek and exploit welfare benefits in societies where they are obtainable.

The Gypsies do not view welfare as charity or aid; rather it is just one more method of outsmarting the non-Gypsy. Since collecting welfare is time-consuming in terms of hours required in agency offices, the Gypsies feel justified in being compensated for the income they lose while waiting. Additionally, since welfare agencies put restrictions on the Gypsies and the Gypsies have to "earn" their money by playing the role of a welfare recipient in a believable fashion, they feel they are justified in accepting the welfare benefits. Moreover, the Gypsies are not a welfare class dependent on governmental support; welfare is just one additional method of obtaining money. They combine welfare with three or four other enterprises to contribute to the support of an extended family.

Nomadism

Gypsies have been nomads ever since they arrived in the Middle East and Europe. However, the underlying causes of the Gypsies' nomadic nature suffer from popular misconceptions: many observers feel they are either too captivated by uncontrollable wanderlust or too lazy to settle down at regular jobs. In reality, the primary motivation behind the Gypsies' frequent movement is their drive to exploit new markets for their skills and services after present markets have been depleted.

Many sources of the Gypsies' wherewithal stem from irregularities and gaps in the supply and demand of the host society. These economic opportunities are occasional, uneven, and seasonal. For the Gypsies to survive, they have accepted this commercial challenge and have developed travel patterns which allow them to exploit these opportunities to the maximum and then move on. Nomadism, an aggressive form of commercial behavior, has enabled the Gypsies to survive in situations where other groups would have failed.

Nomadism has enabled the Gypsies to develop both a winter and summer economy. During the summer it is typical for Gypsies to work at vacation and recreation places and special events, such as Appleby and Epsom fairs in England, as fortunetellers, entertainers, and hawkers of charms and souvenirs (Adams et al. 1975:144; Harvey and Jackson 1973:20, 168–69). Another summer industry for the Gypsies is crop-picking, usually lasting not more than several weeks. However, the Gypsies will accept casual farm work only if they are allowed to work and live together as a group separate from other farm laborers and be paid for their labor on a piece rate basis. In this way they work more as independent contractors than wage laborers (Adams et al. 1975:126; McLaughlin 1980:49; San Roman 1975:177; Sutherland 1975b:90–91).

During the winter, obviously, the Gypsies often limit their traveling to local circuits in more densely populated areas. Used car dealing, blacktopping driveways, body and fender work, collecting scrap metal and rags are all forms of winter work. Fortunetelling is a constant source of income in both the summer and winter economies.

Gypsies I know in Los Angeles travel extensively in search of profitable markets. One *kumpania* spends the fall and winter months in Mexico showing old cowboy films in rural areas. In August when the heat becomes unbearable for them, they travel to Belize and concentrate on fortunetelling; they rent air-conditioned hotel rooms and launch radio campaigns to advertise the clairvoyant abilities of "Madame Ludmilia." The campaign is so successful that people line up outside the hotel to have their palms read. The Gypsies estimate that they see two thousand customers each August. Madame Ludmilia explained: "I could never make a full-time living in Belize if I lived there all year—the country is too small and too poor. But when I show up in August, I am a novelty. I enjoy sitting in an air-conditioned hotel telling fortunes. Why should I sweat my ass off in Oaxaco [Mexico], showing cowboy movies?" Other Los Angeles-based Gypsy *kumpanias* travel to Alaska in the summer to capitalize on the tourist industry. Alaska was added to the Gypsies' travel schedule during the construction of the pipeline. During 1975 and 1978, Valdez, the terminus of the pipeline, served as a rich source of economic opportunities.

In her study of California Gypsies, Sutherland describes a typical winter-summer work agenda:

> In Barvale, many families were on welfare the year round but spent several months in summer camping in fields and picking crops along with other migrant labourers, for extra income. One group of Kuneshti families set up a circuit between San Francisco and Hawaii. They spent the summer in San Francisco where they established residence and received welfare cheques, supplemented by occasional trips to engage in farm labour. In the autumn they would fly to Hawaii where they were able to make a good living at fortune-telling. The occasional *bujo*[1] helped them to get their tickets back to the mainland. In one lean year they did not earn enough in the fields to get to Hawaii and were forced to spend the winter in San Francisco (1975b:48–49).

Gypsy migrations can be quite extensive, depending upon the opportunities that present themselves; for example, San Roman describes the Gypsy colony in La Alegria, Spain (1975:169–99). During harvest time, families travel to Castile and to the south of France to work in the vineyards. When they are not picking, members hawk homemade baskets in the local markets. Upon returning to La Alegria, the women prepare for the winter months by collecting osier twigs to make the baskets they will later sell in the markets. Some of the younger men obtain work as "extras" in western movies that are filmed in Spain. The Gypsy men like this type of work because they are good jockeys, can control how much they work on a particular film, and have the chance to bring other members of their *kumpania* into the production. Other Gypsy men in La Alegria buy tickets to Central and South America—especially Peru, Argentina,

Venezuela, and Mexico—with the money earned during harvest. The usual sojourn in these countries ranges from three months to two years. In these countries, the Spanish Gypsies arrange to live and work with relatives, who show them how to sell to the local populations.

The purpose of these sojourns is to earn money quickly and return to Spain able to afford an improved standard of living there. Upon returning to Spain, the traveler usually buys a flat or house, a car for business purposes, and invests the remainder of the money earned in merchandise like cloth, iron, and watches, which he and his family can sell in Spanish markets. San Roman (1975:177) points out that it is extremely rare for these Gypsies to remain permanently in the Americas.

Some Gypsy travel circuits are shorter than the two described above. In the course of my fieldwork, I interviewed two Gypsy families in the state of Virginia who operated fortunetelling and used car and boat businesses during most of the year, but traveled to rural parts of the state from mid-July to the end of September. One family supplemented work as musicians and dancers for tourists in the Luray Caverns in the Shenandoah State Park with fortunetelling.[2] The other family traveled from one country fair to another in the southern part of the state, working as fortunetellers and entertainers; the itinerary included the Pork, Pine, and Peanut Festival in Surrey County, a predominantly black fair.

In my interview with the city attorney for Williamsburg, Virginia,[3] I confirmed the information given me by one of the Gypsy families I interviewed:

> I was born in Chase City, Virginia. My father was the country doctor there. That's tobacco country. I make a visit back home every summer during the Chase County Fair. Last summer I was shocked to see Mr. Johnson [the husband of the Williamsburg fortuneteller] at the fair working as an organ grinder with a monkey. I know Mr. Johnson from Williamsburg because every year he comes to my office to renew his wife's fortunetelling permit. I wanted to take his picture with the monkey, but he asked me not to.

By being nomadic the Gypsies can remain self-employed and masters of their own destinies while moving from one commercial opportunity to another. A sedentary existence would force them, over time, to accept marginal wage labor from the host society, resulting in the loss of their entrepreneurial edge.

Exploiting Natural Resources or Resources Viewed as Worthless by Society

In their attempt to earn a living in the worst of circumstances, the Gypsies have learned to manufacture products from free materials. Historically, the Gypsies' nomadic life has given them the opportunity to learn about the natural environment and explore the uses of things found in it. Thus, the Gypsies' ability to make something out of nothing is a tremendous advantage to them in the marketplace; it has enabled them to cut drastically the cost of their overhead for items they manufacture—the only cost is family labor. These raw materials that the Gypsies utilize are free because they are deemed worthless by others. Over the centuries, the Gypsies have demonstrated a great deal of cleverness in figuring out what they could manufacture out of worthless material and selling it in finished form to members of the host society.

In Yugoslavia, Gypsies in the Kosovo and Metohija regions eke out a living by manufacturing clay pots and pans and selling them to the Yugoslavs (Vukanović 1961:35–44). The Gypsies adopted this niche from Albanian and Serb inhabitants of these regions who gave up the endeavor when it was no longer profitable for them. The Albanian and Serb earthenware makers could only produce one hundred pots and pans a year, not sufficient to support them. When the Gypsies gradually moved into this niche, neither the Albanians nor the Serbs were threatened because the trade had become passé and unprofitable to them.

By adapting their own commercial techniques to this enterprise, the Gypsies have been able to turn pot-and-pan manufacturing into a viable business venture. Since the Gypsies extract the clay used in the production of the earthenware themselves, the clay costs them nothing. The clay is then transported by the Gypsies to their village, where the entire family is involved in processing and fashioning it into a finished product.

Once the earthenware is ready for sale, adult members of the extended family take it to local and distant towns on market day.

Home production eliminates the need either to hire labor or rent factory space. Thus, the Gypsies vertically control the entire manufacturing process from the extraction of clay from the earth to the sale of the pots and pans on market day; this procedure contributes to keeping their production costs to a minimum. The Gypsies in these regions of Yugoslavia, presently producing three hundred pots and pans a year, consider their business successful.

Gypsies in Romania and Hungary employ similar business methods by manufacturing bricks and rush mats; again, these materials are obtained for nothing. In addition, gypsies in both countries use soft woods, gathered for nothing, to manufacture wooden objects, such as spoons, bowls, children's toys, scrubbing boards, trunks, chests, and replacement parts for looms (Block 1939:155). In the United States today, Gypsies in Washington and South Carolina haul odd pieces of uncut lumber from logging camps for a fee and then make picnic furniture to sell.

For more than a century, English Gypsies have manufactured wooden pegs (clothespins) from small pieces of wood they collect around their caravan sites (Adams et al. 1975:124). Vesey-FitzGerald described the manufacturing process of pegs by English Gypsies.

> Peg-making is not necessarily a one-man job. Nearly always it is the man who makes the pegs and the woman who takes them with her when she goes hawking, and certainly the man never hawks them. I know one south country family who all combine in the making of Pegs. It is an industry with them, and they have reduced it to a fine art in which each member of the family is a specialist, a cog in one great peg-making machine (Vesey-FitzGerald 1973:196).

English, Welsh, Irish, and Scottish Gypsies continue to exploit the natural countryside for heather, gathered and hawked by women and children for "good luck" to non-Gypsies on the main streets of many British cities and towns and fairs. Around Christmastime, they gather holly to sell to non-Gypsies. A Midlands Gypsy woman describes how adept the Gypsies are in making the natural environment a never-ending source of income: "One year was a bad 'un for berries [holly] and the markets was looking for good holly. We got some dried peas, painted them red, then stuck a pin in each and pinned them on the twigs. We took the 'holly' to the market and a man said he'd buy the lot" (Adams et al. 1975:134).

The Gypsy practice of extracting free raw materials from the natural environment for manufacturing has evolved into the ability to make a living from things the dominant society discards. The two prime examples of this practice are scrap metal and rag collection. Both British and Swedish Gypsies have found extremely lucrative niches by collecting and selling waste scrap (Adams et al. 1975:116–21; Gustafsson 1973:20, 23, 91; Okely 1975:56; Takman 1976:96–98). In both Britain and Sweden, the Gypsies are paid a fee to haul scrap metal from factories and homes in the form of outdated machinery, washing machines, stoves, refrigerators, and old cars. They fill a gap in both economies since there is no systematic service for the removal of junk scrap (Civic Trust, 1967–68:81–87). Wise to the value of the junk, the Gypsies first dismantle the items for any valuable metals, like copper and aluminum; then they take the bulk metal of little value and sell it to scrap yards.

Living off the countryside, Gypsies in Britain and Sweden claim abandoned cars and "break" them for the scrap metals. Both men and women assist, removing all the resaleable spare parts. The radiator and battery are stripped for copper and lead, the engine and gearbox for cast iron, and the chassis and axles for heavy steel. The remainder of the car, made of light iron, is scrapped at a junkyard (Adams et al. 1975:118). In the course of their scrap collecting, the Gypsies often come across a car, stove, refrigerator, or other item which can be sold after minor repairs. Scrap metal collection is widespread among the British Gypsies: it is estimated that 93 percent of the men and 51 percent of the women are engaged in it (Adams et al. 1975:119).

Rag collection, predominantly a woman's activity, is another Gypsy occupation which has evolved from living off the natural environment. Gypsy women obtain rags by going door to door with a baby buggy and begging for "hand-me-downs" for their family. Owing to *marime* codes, the women have no intention of allowing any member of their family to wear the clothes that the *gaje* have given them, but instead the better clothing items are resold intact to second-hand clothing dealers and the rest are sold to cotton rag and woolen dealers. Adams and her associates (1975:119) estimate that 51 percent of all Gypsy women in the British Isles are engaged in the collection and sale of rags and woolens.

Avoiding Sex-Typing in Work

The Gypsies have also adapted to adverse circumstances by avoiding rigid distinctions between the sexes regarding work. Certainly there are occupations which, over time, have become predominantly male or female. For example, fortunetelling is always women's work, and the buying and selling of used cars is almost always men's work; the Gypsies have learned through experience that one or the other sex is more successful at a particular enterprise. There are no cultural assumptions on the Gypsies' part of what denotes male and female work roles—only commercial ones. Consequently, one rule governs: the most lucrative enterprise deserves top priority.

In order to be financially successful, the Gypsies work together as an economic unit. They have developed a highly fluid work force in which members of the extended family are constantly changing roles and responsibilities to accommodate the opportunity which offers the highest degree of money-making potential. As a result, it is not an uncommon sight to see Gypsy women involved in what the host society would label "men's work" or for men to be involved in "women's work." In fact, the Gypsies' notion of appropriate work for men and women and children is often the reverse of what the dominant society views as appropriate. In many endeavors, the women and children are given the most dirty and arduous tasks, while the men take on considerably easier tasks (Sutherland 1975b:90; Vukanović 1961:39).

If a woman's fortunetelling business is doing well, her husband, father-in-law, mother-in-law, brother-in-law, and children will reduce their own money-making activities to assist her in her business. This situation does not embarrass her husband; rather, it makes him proud. In the labor structure of a fortunetelling operation, the fortuneteller is the most visible member of the work team, but she is only the tip of the iceberg. Behind the scenes the members of her extended family all help to make her business venture successful. In essence, the fortuneteller is a performer who overcommunicates her "Gypsiness" so that her customers will believe she is clairvoyant. The other members of the work team undercommunicate their "Gypsiness"; they have the responsibilities of maintaining the fortunetelling parlor, advertising, obtaining customers, and paying rent, license fees, and bribes to officials, as well as providing general relief—e.g., caring for younger children, cooking, cleaning—for the fortuneteller so she can be free to earn money.

Indeed, childcare often becomes a male responsibility. Since children are considered a nuisance at a fortunetelling parlor, they spend long hours with their fathers, uncles, and grandfathers. Typically the children accompany the men wherever they go—on body and fender jobs, shopping, and visiting other Gypsies. When a Gypsy child is ill, often the father acts as nurturer, tending the child's needs and chauffeuring him or her to doctor and dental appointments. This revealing statement was made by a thirteen-year-old Gypsy girl suffering from an abscessed tooth: "Last night my father stayed up with me the whole night, I was in so much pain." When asked why her mother had not stayed with her instead, she told me: "My mother works hard in her business [fortunetelling]; she needs her sleep." Conversely, in situations where the man in the family has found the most profitable niche, the family work force will rearrange and work to accommodate him and his commercial needs. Thus, as in the case of the Yugoslav Gypsies who manufacture earthenware, it is the women and the children who work the hardest by stamping on the unprocessed clay with their bare feet in order to make it malleable enough to be shaped into pots (Vukanović 1961:39).

The case of the "traveling cinema" in Mexico provides another interesting example of Gypsy women assisting their husbands' business endeavors. Currently there are several large *kumpanias* traveling throughout Mexico showing old cowboy movies to inhabitants of the hinterlands (see Pickett 1965:87–94). These Spanish-speaking Gypsies who travel with the *cine ambulante* in Mexico have shrewdly responded to the demand to bring movie entertainment to remote areas of the country. Given their keen understanding of the Mexican economy, they strategically plot visits to places where workers have money from copper mining, oil fields, or harvest. As might be imagined, approaching these areas is often difficult—poor roads, bandits, bribe-hungry policemen, and a number of other dangers. For these reasons, the Gypsies in Mexico travel in groups of two or more extended families for support and protection. They must bring everything with them, including their own power generators run by kerosene or diesel.

Depending on the wealth of these families, a traveling movie operation can be quite luxurious, complete with neon lights, glass-encased poster holders, expensive projectors, and even an extra trailer with benchlike seats for the spectators (Pickett 1965:88). Many of these better-equipped operations have huge tents made of tarpaulin sewn together to create an enclosure which can seat many people.[4] These operations also have jeeps used to carry a projector, screen, and a small power plant into even more inaccessible areas (Pickett 1965:91). Poorer family groups with less equipment often bribe a local mayor and set up the movie at a rural schoolhouse, using the whitewashed exterior wall as a screen (Pickett 1965:91).

The Gypsies advertise the movies by playing music over loudspeakers to attract the attention of the villagers (Pickett 1965:91). In larger towns, trucks are driven through the main streets with music playing, and performances are announced by shouting into a microphone hooked onto the record player. The women complete the advertising campaign by going into town on foot to tell the potential patrons about the movie. In addition to advertising for the cinema, the women perform many other duties contributing to the overall success of the business.

Pickett, who studied and traveled with the *Rom* in Mexico, describes the flexibility this group exhibits in dividing work responsibilities between the sexes:

It is obvious that the traveling movie is a family or group operation which functions under extremely difficult conditions and demands full cooperation of each member of the group in order to be successful. For this reason, a rigid and strict division of labor between the sexes is somewhat unpractical [sic]. In general, the men among the group are responsible for setting up, operating, and maintaining the movie equipment, obtaining the films, driving and maintaining the vehicles, and performing any heavy manual labor necessary in setting up a camp. Among these groups which practice metal-working in addition to operating a movie, the men also take charge of this. The women care for the young, secure and prepare food, and include fortune-telling, shop-lifting and the like among their duties and are also responsible for washing clothes and the general cleanliness of the trucks and camp, in addition to making clothes for themselves and their children, mending, making and repairing the *ceranda* (quilts) and airing them, and in general assisting the men and running errands for them whenever necessary. The young of both sexes assist wherever they are needed. This is a general breakdown of the division of labor and it is not uncommon to see a man cook or sweep, nor would he be considered less of a *Rom* for doing so (Pickett 1965:93).

Pickett rightly observes the impracticality of "rigid and strict division of labor between the sexes"; consequently, Gypsy society regards appropriate work for men and women in a completely different manner.

Avoiding Age Barriers

When dividing labor, the Gypsies disregard age much as they do gender. According to the Gypsy philosophy, every member of the *kumpania* should contribute to its economic success, regardless of his or her age. While children and elderly people may enjoy a reduced schedule in money-making activities, they are required to contribute something to the group. Even in cases of infirmity due to illness or extreme old age, a Gypsy can earn income for the *kumpania* through welfare or some other type of passive employment.

Through a process which begins very early in life Gypsy children are socialized to become shrewd business people. Children spend most of their waking hours accompanying their parents, older siblings, or grandparents on business ventures. In this way the children learn an occupation while also being trained how to bargain, how to handle themselves, and how to avoid being cheated in a marketplace situation. Gypsy children are encouraged to develop a strong and forceful personality which will give them the upper hand in business dealings (Gustafsson 1973:93–94).

Often children assist in family businesses, performing tasks that require less skill and allowing older and more skilled adults to concentrate on the most difficult part of the operation. For example, children accompanying males of the *kumpania* on body and fender expeditions are constantly on the lookout for cars with dents. The children report their "finds" to older males who often are able to obtain jobs this way. While the older males are repairing the automobile, the children comb the neighborhood for other jobs. A ten-year-old Kalderash boy in Los Angeles reveals how the Gypsies rely upon children in this way:

Saturday was a bad day. Me, my father, and brother drove down all the streets in Glendale, Monrovia, and Highland Park look-

ing for body and fender work. My father was really getting up-
set. He said to me, "This is a waste of gas. I don't see any cars
that need fixing." So I tried real hard, and I noticed a car with a
dent in the back parked in someone's driveway. I told my father
to stop the car. I ran out and knocked on the door and asked the
man if we could fix his car for $20. He said, "OK." My father
was so happy he gave me $5 for getting him the job.

Moreover, in situations like the manufacturing of pots and pans in
the Kosovo region in Yugoslavia, Gypsy children stamp the clay
(Vukanović 1961:39). And they are regularly used in farm labor
(Adams et al. 1975:126; McLaughlin 1980:49; San Roman 1975:177;
Sutherland 1975b:72, 89–91).

In addition to being auxiliary labor, children often perform in minor business ventures that adults find either undesirable or more
profitable in the hands of children. Begging is the best example of
this child industry; child beggars can earn far more in a day than
adults. Children are also more successful at hawking some items,
such as real or handmade flowers. Whereas an adult would need a
business license to sell flowers or other small items outside a department store like Macy's in New York or San Francisco, children
are likely to be overlooked by authorities. In an interview with three
San Francisco Gypsy children, twelve years old and under, who sell
fresh flowers at a major tourist attraction every night during the
summer, the children said they averaged seventy dollars a night between them for four hours work of hawking. American Gypsies have
learned to let their children sell these items on weekends and after
school hours so as not to provoke the curiosity of the police or any
other officials.

Gypsy children also contribute economically to the *kumpania*
through welfare benefits. Since many Gypsies collect welfare benefits, it is not surprising that they know the welfare rules thoroughly.
In the United States, Gypsy women handle welfare matters because
they have learned about Aid to Families with Dependent Children
(AFDC). Consequently, the majority of Gypsies applying for welfare
are women with four to nine children whose husbands have "abandoned" them. In social welfare departments where the social workers investigate Gypsy cases carefully and demand that all claimed
children be regularly accounted for, the Gypsies "adopt" children
from other parts of the state or from other states.

Similarly, old people contribute to the income of the extended family through their ability to collect special welfare benefits. For example, any person living in California who is over sixty-five and has no income is eligible for Old Age Security (OAS). If they are physically disabled—including health problems such as obesity, heart disease, and diabetes—they are entitled to Aid to the Totally Dependent (ATD). And if an old person can claim not to be able to read an eye chart upon medical examination, he or she can collect Blind Aid.

The welfare benefits reaped by children and old people in one extended family can provide from $600 to $1400 a month. The following is a monthly welfare benefit sheet for one Gypsy family in central California:[5]

$142.00	ATD to head of household for obesity, diabetes, and heart trouble
180.00	Blind Aid to wife
221.00	AFDC to daughter-in-law with three children
114.00	For an adult son with cerebral palsy
148.00	AFDC for an adult daughter and child
$805.00	Total

In a sense this monthly allowance can be called passive employment on the part of the Gypsies. In reality, few Gypsy families have been deserted by the father and husband. Children, old, and disabled Gypsies are economically productive despite the stories they tell their social workers.

In fact, largely because the non-Gypsies do not understand the economic role Gypsy children play in their society, Gypsy schools established by non-Gypsies frequently fail. The chief complaint by administrators of Gypsy schools is the high rate of absenteeism among their students (in the United States, Tyrnauer 1977:43–48; in Sweden, Gustafsson 1973:84–92 and Takman 1976:86–90). Gypsy parents often enroll their children in school because welfare benefits are tied to school attendance. The Gypsy parents see no problem with this since the child is enabling the family to earn money through welfare benefits; however, if other economic opportunities for the child occur, the parents see nothing wrong in removing the child from school so they can exploit them. Because welfare benefits are often tied to school attendance, Gypsy children are often used as pawns by their parents. In discussing some of the events that took place at a Gypsy school in Stockholm, Gustafsson wrote: "Some parents even use their children's school attendance in bargaining for favors: 'If the Social Welfare Board will not pay for a new sofa the children will not be allowed to go to school.' Or, 'The children will not be allowed to go to school until we get a new flat' " (Gustafsson 1973:88).

In analyzing the difficulties of the Gypsy school, Gustafsson mentioned that children would be gone for months at a time to travel with their parents. One boy of twelve was absent for a long period of time because he had been with his father buying and selling used cars (p. 89). Three children from another Gypsy family demonstrated "dismal attendance" because their parents expected adult responsibilities of them: "The elder boy is a skillful assistant to his father, who deals in cars, and has begun to consider starting his own business in scrap copper from houses being demolished. The 14-year-old girl now and again takes care of the house and a younger, ailing brother for days on end. The ten-year-old boy earned 200 Swedish kroner in a couple of hours at a fair one summer" (Gustafsson 1973:91). In another study of Gypsies in Sweden, Takman (1976) observed that even school-aged children contributed to the economy of the household: "The children sell tickets at the entrance of the amusement camps, run the shooting gallery, collect junk, and beat the drum in the orchestra" (Takman 1976:90).

In concluding her study on the Gypsy School of Stockholm, Gustafsson could not separate the failure of the school from the economic demands placed on the children by their parents and the other members of the Gypsy community. Gustafsson concluded her report on the Gypsy School:

> That the old pattern according to which the occupation is taught by father to son still exists. That the growing years of children are still not really understood (by the parents) as a long non-specialized period of preparation, as in the majority society. That children in a Gypsy family still have an economic role is not unique. It is really only very recently in highly industrialized societies that members of a family have only an emotional function towards one another (Gustafsson, 1973:89–90).

Like children, older Gypsies are expected to contribute to the *kumpania.* Often because of failing health, older Gypsy men and women act as overseers or supervisors of businesses while younger

Gypsies perform the more strenuous tasks. For example, I interviewed an eighty-two-year-old Kalderash man who runs traveling cinema operations in Mexico and Puerto Rico. He oversees four operations at once, employing sons, nephews, and grandchildren to do all of the difficult work. This elderly man performs the less strenuous tasks of traveling to Los Angeles to buy old cowboy movies, tents, clothing, and anything else the *kumpania* needs.

Adams, Okely, Morgan, and Smith (1975) found that the concept of formal retirement among the Gypsies is unknown (p. 138). They describe a women in her seventies who went out "calling" every morning with a pram selling "lucky" black cats, collecting rags, telling fortunes, and inquiring about scrap metal for her son. This book also mentions an old Gypsy man in his seventies who maintains his lucrative contracts, collects scrap from several factories every few weeks, and occasionally engages in light scrap-breaking (p. 138).

Such economic contribution among the Gypsies is both a responsibility and a privilege. Avoidance of age barriers in the distribution of labor has contributed to the Gypsies' success as a group.

Being Multioccupational

It has become a business principle among the Gypsies never to depend upon one occupation. Since so many of the Gypsies' occupations are seasonal, temporary, marginal, and even precarious, they engage in a number of endeavors simultaneously. Every member of a *kumpania* commonly derives an income from two or more occupations or businesses at the same time. For example, in the United States, Gypsy men glean a living through body and fender work, used car dealing, farm labor, entertainment, and promoting their wives', mothers', sisters', and daughters-in-law's fortunetelling businesses. Women tell fortunes, collect welfare, sell on the street, perform farm labor, and entertain. Children of both sexes earn money through attending school (i.e., ensuring welfare benefits for the family), begging, selling on the street, engaging in farm labor, and entertaining; in addition, children are used as auxiliary labor in any adult business.

Being multioccupational seems to be a universal Gypsy practice. In his survey of Swedish Gypsies, Takman (1976:91–96) discusses his difficulty in organizing data on Gypsy occupations because they were simultaneously engaged in so many of them. Takman found that Swedish Gypsy men were most commonly engaged as junk dealers, used car dealers, musicians, retinners and coppersmiths, and "free professionals" who manufactured and sold brushes and shoes. Takman noted that the Gypsy men were self-employed in a variety of businesses at once, often conducting their operations on the street in a vacant lot. Furthermore, Takman found the same multioccupational behavior among the Gypsy women, 70 percent of whom worked regularly. The women juggled the occupations of amusement camp worker, musician, dancer, and fortuneteller.

Adams, Okely, Morgan, and Smith found that "a multiplicity of occupations was both valued and practiced by the vast majority of Gypsies in England" (1975:132). In that study, the wealthiest and most successful families were those with the greatest spread of occupations. Most Gypsies whom Adams and her associates studied took pride in being able to turn adverse circumstances into profitable ones; they frequently boasted: "You could put me down anywhere in the world and I could earn a living. You could even put me in a desert" (Adams et al. 1975:132).

The practice of being multioccupational affords the Gypsies a peculiar form of job security. Since the Gypsies never rely on one mode of work, they are never without a means to earn a living. If a particular market closes to them because it has been exhausted or they have been harassed by the police, they can quickly turn to other methods of earning a living. This occupational flexibility and pluralism should be viewed as a result of years of economic adaptation to unfriendly and unreliable market situations. The Gypsy practice of diversity enables them to survive the harshest of economic circumstances.

CONCLUSION

As a middleman minority dogged by great antipathy, the Gypsies have demonstrated an amazing degree of ingenuity in adapting to host environments in forty different countries of the world. As a group, the *Rom* have become economically successful even though they are illiterate and lack educated professionals among them to serve as advocates in times of crisis. Despite their inability to read and write, the Gypsies have a keen understanding of the land and people where they dwell and work. The Gypsies have certainly proved their ability to make a living even under the most dismal of conditions.

The romantic image of the Gypsies as carefree wanderers quickly disappears when one realizes the sacrifices they must make for group survival. Nomadism is not a sign of the Gypsies' wanderlust; it is an economic practice which has enabled them to seize opportunities and exploit them to the fullest. As nomads, the *Rom* are ready to satisfy gaps, shortages, and irregularities in various economies. Through their travels, Gypsies have learned to live from the land and consequently have developed the clever ability to manufacture commercial products from free natural resources: the Gypsies can make something from nothing and sell it at a fine profit.

Adversity has caused the Gypsies to work hard as a group. This has led them to use all the available labor they can get, and every member of the *kumpania* must therefore contribute. The Gypsies do not have the luxury of dividing work by sex or age, and children and old people must perform necessary tasks.

Moreover, the *Rom* have learned that it is dangerous to specialize in one occupation. During their history they lost the ability to earn a living because either their occupations became obsolete, such as coppersmithing and bellmaking, or host prejudices became too great. Adapting to this uncertainty, the Gypsies have become multi-occupational, developing semiskills in a variety of occupations and professions. If every member of the *kumpania* has two or more methods of earning a living, it becomes less likely that the group will ever suffer from lack of work or business opportunities.

In sum, Gypsies, like other middleman minorities, are successful because they rely on family labor, intraethnic cooperation, a dual ethic, and a hard work ethos which gives them the competitive edge over members of the various host societies where they dwell and work. Additionally, the Gypsies exceed typical middleman economic behavior and employ at least five extra measures which assist them in being successful. Given these five measures, the Gypsies emerge as a middleman minority par excellence.

Chapter 8

CONCLUSION

N THE SECOND chapter of this study, I raised a key question: is it necessary for the social system to remain structurally the same for middleman minorities to maintain their interstitial position? Blalock (1967:79–84) asserts that the persistence of middleman minority groups requires lack of change in the social and economic structure in which they dwell.

> Though it is perhaps true that most minorities are low-status groups, there are some that occupy intermediate positions owing to a competitive advantage or a high adaptive capacity. Such minorities are often associated with special occupational niches by virtue of a combination of circumstances, plus a cultural heritage that has been used as an adaptive mechanism over a prolonged period. As long as the social system remains structurally the same, these groups often become "perpetual" minorities, whereas minorities that are initially less fortunate may eventually become completely absorbed into the dominant group (Blalock 1967:79–80).

Conversely, Bonacich (1973) has observed that these groups "persist beyond the status gap" (p. 584), but no other scholars in the field of middleman minority theory have seriously challenged Blalock's proposition. I believe the major contribution of this study is its demonstration that Gypsies endure as a middleman minority despite the most radical economic and social structural changes in any society.

Gypsy Middlemen

Gypsies functioned as middlemen in preindustrial Europe and have remained in that position until the present, operating with moderate success in advanced capitalist, socialist, and communist societies. Gypsies have the remarkable ability to move successfully between various types of economies. A good illustration of this movement between differing economies is illustrated in chapter 6 with the example of the Yugoslav Gypsies abandoned in the Arizona desert.

This band of 102 non-English-speaking Gypsies came to the United States from Yugoslavia, an eastern European communist country; none of these Gypsies had lived or worked in a capitalist society before. Despite their unfamiliarity with the language and economy and their totally illegal immigration status in this country, they managed to remain here and thrive economically.

This group's victory over extremely serious immigration and re-settlement problems was accomplished in two ways. In the first place, their American coethnics accepted total responsibility for su-pervising their resettlement. This process involved finding an eco-nomic niche for the Yugoslav Gypsies somewhere in America that would not interfere with another Gypsy group's livelihood. In addi-tion to finding the Yugoslav Gypsies a place to live and work, the American Gypsy leadership provided them with the shrewd advice that prevented their deportation from this country and eventually permitted their permanent residency. In the second place, the Yu-goslav Gypsies were adaptable. Settled in a poor and predominantly black and Hispanic neighborhood in Chicago, these Gypsies turned an economically depressed area into a lucrative fortunetelling dis-trict with three *ofisa* locations. Two weeks after their resettlement in Chicago, the women of this tribe knew enough English to give cursory palm readings. Now, some fourteen years after their arrival, they have purchased much of the real estate in their territory, mar-ried their children into powerful American Gypsy families, and implanted themselves into American soil legally, socially, and economically.[1]

Clearly these Gypsies from a communist society possess all the typical middleman business skills, although they have spent almost their entire lives under a regime which ideologically, legally, and economically discourages private enterprise and entrepreneurship. The rapid adaptation of the Yugoslav Gypsies in Chicago suggests that possibly their middleman business skills were not destroyed by living and working in a society which outlaws and condemns such skills. The Gypsies have always combated adversity through adapt-ability. The plain fact that Gypsies continue to function in com-munist societies as self-employed business people reveals a stub-born attachment to the middleman way of life. The Yugoslav Gypsies prove the point.

Other examples in chapter 7 suggest that middleman business

practices are widespread in eastern European communist societies. The pot and pan manufacturers and sellers of the Kosovo-Methohija region endure as do the manufacturers and sellers of bricks and mats in Rumania and Hungary. Self-employment in the eastern European countries often takes the form of selling shish kebabs on the street, shining shoes, or working as a musician or dancer.[2]

In the Soviet Union, Gypsy entertainment arts are appreciated, and a certain percentage of the Gypsy population there can earn a living by selling their talents.[3] Many of the leading musical celebrities in the Soviet Union and Hungary are Gypsies. The Soviet government has nurtured and supported the Gypsy theater, *Romen*, in Moscow since the 1930s (Malnick 1959:84). In all of the eastern European communist societies, Gypsies work as fortunetellers and folk healers; however, these endeavors operate covertly. Despite its lowly status, begging is another form of self-employment. I am not arguing that Gypsies become wealthy through these endeavors in communist countries, but by engaging in them they circumvent the system's pressure to work as wage laborers.

No matter how well planned and centralized a communist economy is, there will always be gaps that the Gypsies can fill. Socialism and communism have not destroyed the citizens' thirst for exotic music, dancing, and "prophecy." It is important to keep in mind that many of the countries I mentioned are still populated with superstitious people among whom the myth of Gypsy magic workers still persists. Regarded as an epiphenomenon of the decaying capitalist epoch, the Gypsies remain an ideological embarrassment to eastern European communist leaders who have been unable to coax them into a sedentary rank-and-file-worker existence (Gilliat-Smith 1948; Koudelka 1975; Puxon 1969, 1976; Rosenthal 1959; Ulč 1969; Vukanović 1961).

While Gypsies from a communist society can fit very well into a capitalist society, it is also true that Gypsies from a highly developed capitalist society can succeed quite well economically in a less developed Third World country. This has been demonstrated by the American Kalderash Gypsies who operate the traveling cinema in Mexico. The level of development is so low in many of the regions where the Gypsies venture, they must equip themselves completely. Each traveling cinema group is a twentieth-century self-sustaining unit complete with a small power plant, projector, screen, audio equipment, and microphone, operating in the undeveloped heartlands of Mexico and Central America (Pickett, 1965, 1966a, 1966b).

Movement back and forth between various types of economic systems does not cause the Gypsies much hardship. The Gypsies have the capacity to exploit certain economic opportunities regardless of the structure of the society. Even though the social and economic structure of a society changes, the Gypsies remain a middleman minority. From their middleman position they overcome any structural reorganization with increased diversity and adaptability. The Gypsies prove that Blalock's assertion does not hold up under careful examination. Despite major structural changes in any economic system, the Gypsies survive, intact, as a middleman minority. They are not absorbed into the camp of wage earners, and they continue to engage in entrepreneurial activities which, if necessary, they will do covertly. What accounts for this fierce retention of the middleman status and way of life is an uncompromised cultural heritage, coupled with tightly regulated business practices.

Ethnocentrism

Gypsies are extremely ethnocentric. Their belief in and adherence to *marime* codes serve as the strongest barrier between them and all other peoples. This fundamental force prevents Gypsies from interacting with non-Gypsies in any significant way and communally insures against assimilation. *Marime* also establishes the basis for a dual ethic. It dictates that contact between Gypsies and non-Gypsies be strictly limited to business dealings. To interact with non-Gypsies in any way other than in a strictly business fashion is to invite the suspicion and hostility of the entire group. Non-Gypsies are, by definition, *marime*. Social or sexual intercourse with them results in excommunication from the ethnic group.

Another religious belief which has, in effect, maintained group cohesion and prevented serious conflict from becoming violent is the Gypsies' belief in ghosts. As noted in chapter 4, this belief is a strong deterrent against committing murder. The belief in and fear of ghosts extends to non-Gypsies as well. Consequently, Gypsies are a nonviolent group. In light of their small numbers and powerless social position, their nonviolence has made them less threatening to the dominant group. In an external sense, nonviolence has been adaptive. Internally, the belief in and fear of ghosts has preserved the ethnic group. It curtails any extremely abusive behavior between Gypsies. Ethnic vice aimed at members of one's own group, like "protection rackets" or contract murder, is nonexistent among the Gypsies.

The ramifications of the 1947 Mexico City shoot-out cited in chapter 4 illustrate the dire and lasting consequences that result when one Gypsy kills another. Like the Jewish concept of building a hedge around the Torah, in which a series of concentric lesser laws are established to prevent a transgression of a major law, the Gypsy belief in ghosts prevents them from engaging in any conflict that might lead to murder. Wife beatings, child abuse, fist fights, and other violent behavior hardly exist among Gypsies.

Tribe and Family Ties

Strong adherence to religious beliefs and practices is assured by the Gypsies' extensive tribal and family links. Group solidarity among the Gypsies is reinforced by four separate and interconnected loyalties. Every Gypsy is loyal to his or her nation, *kumpania, vitsa,* and *familia* (extended family). The basic unit of the Gypsy nation is the family. The family, the key socializing force, assures that every Gypsy child will grow up to be a culturally faithful and economically productive Gypsy adult. For this reason, Gypsy children are separated from the non-Gypsy world as much as possible. School attendance is permitted until a Gypsy child is ten or eleven years old; after that, it is prohibited.

Adolescent life is filled with practical occupational training for adulthood, while simultaneously imposing regulations which keep the sexes separated. Dating is forbidden because it is believed to result in premarital sex, pregnancy, and family disgrace. Parents maintain tight control over children of both sexes until marriage. These marriages are always arranged by the parents and extended family members. Arranged marriages afford the Gypsy community control not only over young adults but also over every member of the community. Since marriages are arranged on the basis of family purity, adherence to Gypsy tradition, a solid reputation in the Gypsy community, and industriousness, a form of social selection exists. The families that become the most powerful and gain the most territory carefully observe the dual ethic, exhibit shrewd business skills, and observe ritual purity laws. These families, by refusing to arrange marriages with Gypsy families that cheat other Gypsies, lack business savvy, or create problems in the non-Gypsy community, eventually eliminate the deviants.

A prime example in this elimination process was Steve Tene, the Gypsy who sold his "true story of Gypsy life" to Peter Maas for $50,000 for the book, *King of the Gypsies* (1975). Tene has been condemned *marime* for this act. Consequently, he and his entire *vitsa* is excluded from marriage with other Gypsies. Without marriage in the Gypsy community, economic and social life terminates. In less than one generation, Tene's family will lose their status as true *Rom* and be reduced to marginal outcasts living on the fringes of the *gaje* society. By refusing to contract marriages with proscribed families, the Gypsies eliminate the deviants in their society. Those who will not behave in a true Gypsy fashion in terms of religious observance, group loyalty, and economic practices will be permanently weeded out. By eliminating these deviants, the Gypsies retain and strengthen their religious, cultural, and economic heritage. Instead of these values weakening over time, as is often the case with other middleman groups, the Gypsies become more culturally observant and economically industrious.

Economic Territoriality

Economic territoriality is another feature of Gypsy society which fosters group cohesion. Staking out a territory ensures each Gypsy *kumpania* the opportunity and right to a livelihood; this practice does not ensure every Gypsy the same opportunity, but in a sense this economic safety net provides moderate security. The practice of economic territoriality guarantees a business location undisturbed by competition from other Gypsies. Furthermore, personal initiative, hard work, creativity, and ability to work with family members as a team are the attributes which distinguish the highly successful Gypsies from the others.

Gypsy Justice

Maintenance and regulation of territories is ensured by *romania* and enforced by the ethnic leadership through the *kris*. In practice, the

Gypsies' system of justice is extremely democratic, enhancing group solidarity and ensuring the spirit and intention of *romania*. Thus, Gypsy justice is democratic because all legal disputes are tried within full view of the community. Because the community's responsible participation is welcomed and expected, every Gypsy in the reasonable vicinity (within five hundred miles) is obligated to attend any *kris* proceedings. An additional democratic feature of Gypsy justice is that all men or women must represent themselves; advocates are forbidden. A poor Gypsy will not suffer due to the inability to hire a skilled lawyer. As a safeguard, a wealthy Gypsy cannot have members of his *kumpania* act as judges.

All issues and evidence are discussed openly for the community to hear. There are no secrets in the Gypsy community. The American legal practices of closed sessions, pretrial hearings, plea-bargaining, and out-of-court settlements do not exist in Gypsy law; in fact, these practices are viewed by the Gypsies as underhanded and ultimately unjust.

Since Gypsies have no policemen or jails, punishment is the responsibility of the entire Gypsy community who enforces the verdict decided by the *kris*. For example, if a Gypsy is sentenced *marime*, it is expected that no other Gypsy in the community will conduct business, travel, or even share a meal with him or his family. The penalty for consorting with the guilty party is a *marime* sentence for all those involved and their families. Such collective responsibility for justice and punishment serves two important functions. First, it promotes wide consensus among the Gypsies that justice prevails. Since the democratic legal system is not just controlled by the elites, every Gypsy has the same access to justice, and information is plentiful. The majority of Gypsies firmly believe the system serves them equitably, producing strong group solidarity. Second, making every Gypsy responsible for punishment promotes social control. Accompanied by widespread gossip, public knowledge effectively enforces the verdict by ostracizing lawbreakers. The scorn and public disgrace of this collective action serve as deterrents to others in the community who might consider misconduct.

When community ostracism fails to curb the deviant behavior of the convicted, the Gypsies employ other methods. Chapter 6 provides a detailed analysis of how the Gypsies use non-Gypsy authorities to punish those Gypsies beyond their control. For this reason the leadership of the Gypsy community carefully cultivates relationships with people of power in the *gaje* world. City attorneys, police chiefs, judges, state senators, and social workers are regarded as the best people to befriend for social control purposes. For example, when a renegade Gypsy couple moved into chief George Anders's territory without permission or an obligatory visit of respect and began committing welfare fraud there, he used his friendly relationship with a social worker to expose and punish them within the laws of the welfare department.

Economic Adaptation

This strong cultural foundation cannot be separated from the Gypsies' economic adaptation in virtually every type of economy. Strong host antipathy has forced Gypsies to earn a livelihood under the worst of circumstances. Traditional middleman business practices—the dual ethic, liquidity of assets, rotating credit, and intraethnic cooperation—have not been enough to guarantee Gypsies' economic security. In addition, the Gypsies have added extra measures to their entrepreneurial repertoire for survival. I have identified five extra measures: (a) nomadism; (b) exploitation of natural resources or resources viewed as worthless by the host society; (c) avoidance of sex typing in the division of labor; (d) avoidance of age barriers in the division of labor; and (e) a multioccupational strategy.

Nomadism is a defensive form of commercial behavior. By being nomadic, the Gypsies can freely exploit gaps and irregularities in various host economies. Often they pursue occasional and seasonal markets. In most cases, Gypsies have established winter and summer economies. In the United States, winter work consists of used car dealing, blacktopping driveways, and body and fender work. Summer work consists of crop-picking as independent contractors and entertaining at county fairs and amusement sites. Fortunetelling and collecting welfare benefits are sources of income year round. Nomadism offers Gypsies complete economic freedom. Although they suffer the societal ramifications of not being "tied to the soil," as Simmel would have argued, they also profit from it (Sway 1981:43–44). In a Simmelian sense, it is not in their economic interest to "overcome the freedom of coming and going" (Simmel 1950:402; see also Sway 1981:44–45).

The most ingenious of the Gypsies' extra economic measures is their ability to make something from nothing and then sell it at a profit. The Gypsies' exploitation of natural resources or resources viewed as worthless by the rest of society has made economic survival possible in otherwise impossible situations. It has become the Gypsies' economic practice to extract some material from the host environment, manufacture something marketable, and then sell it to non-Gypsies. All aspects of the production, from start to finish, remain in the hands of the Gypsies. There are notable examples of this activity: in the Kosovo and Metohija regions of Yugoslavia, the *Rom* extract clay from the ground to manufacture earthenware pots and pans (Vukanović 1961:35–44). In Hungary and Rumania, they collect soft wood to fashion into spoons, bowls, and replacement parts for looms (Block 1939:155). For more than a century, English Gypsies have manufactured clothespins from small pieces of wood collected in the forest. These same Gypsies also scour the landscape for heather and holly, sold as "good luck" charms to the *gaje* (Adams et al. 1975:134; Vesey-FitzGerald 1973:196). In the United States, Gypsies are paid a fee to haul from logging camps uncut lumber, which they take and manufacture into picnic furniture.

An extension of the Gypsies' practice of exploiting the natural environment is to collect and recycle items the dominant society views as worthless. This practice has allowed Gypsies in England and Sweden to derive a living from scrap metal and rag collection. As discriminating scavengers, the Gypsies often come across abandoned cars that can be repaired, then sold as operating vehicles. Since there is no government agency in Great Britain to remove and destroy discarded vehicles on the roads, the Gypsies actually perform a needed service for the government while earning a profit at the same time (Civic Trust, 1967–68).

In a similar manner, Gypsies haul undesired refuse from vacant lots, yards, or businesses; they also save, restore, and resell stoves, refrigerators, washing machines, and office equipment. In a widespread practice among British and Swedish Gypsies, what they cannot resell they dismantle for various scrap metals like copper, aluminum, lead, cast iron, heavy metal, and light iron. (Adams et al. 1975:118; Gustafsson 1973: 20–23, 91; Okely 1975:56; Takman 1976:96–98).

Gypsies also use their skills as discriminating scavengers with used clothing. Although they claim they collect it for charity, they resell the usable items to the *gaje* (wholesale to second-hand dealers or directly to the public at a jumble sale or bazaar). What cannot be sold is "ragged" according to its fiber content; the Gypsies divide the unusable clothing into cotton and wool. Much of the wool the Gypsies sell is sent to Italy where it is reprocessed as blankets.[4]

Another way in which the Gypsies have become a middleman minority par excellence is by avoiding sex classification of work. All members of the extended family share work as needed to maximize fully the potential of an economic opportunity. Over time Gypsies have learned that one sex or another is more successful at a particular endeavor. For example, English Gypsy women specialize in collecting used clothes from *gaje* housewives because men would be perceived as too threatening. However, once the clothing is obtained, men and women equally participate in its sorting and wholesale or retail sale. In a reverse situation, English Gypsy men typically haul refuse from a location to their campsite, where they "break" the refuse into valuable metals with their wives, mothers, sisters, sisters-in-law, and daughters. The Gypsies regard rigid division of labor between the sexes as impractical and counterproductive.

Similarly, any division in labor due to age is not practiced. It is the responsibility and privilege of every member of the *kumpania* to contribute financially to the wealth of the group; therefore, the Gypsies use old people and children as integral parts of their economies. There is no concept of retirement among the *Rom*. When group members become too feeble to participate vigorously, they contribute to the *kumpania* through what I term passive employment. Its most frequent source is the collection of welfare benefits. As explained in chapter 7, Gypsies over sixty-five years of age reap welfare benefits in the form of Old Age Security and Blind Aid. In addition, older Gypsies serve as supervisors in business enterprises. Often they care for young or sick children, allowing younger members of the *vitsa* to pursue their business ventures.

Children closely parallel old people in terms of their economic function within the Gypsy community. Children function as auxiliary labor in almost all Gypsy businesses, performing the less complicated tasks so the adults can focus their attention on the more difficult ones. Like old people, children contribute to the *kumpania* through passive employment. Children figure importantly in any welfare collected by the *kumpania*. Often they earn their welfare benefits by attending public school. Moreover, they make convincing props at the welfare office when some female member of their *kumpania* applies for Aid to Families with Dependent Children.

Finally, Gypsy children specialize in their own industries. Gypsies learned centuries ago that dirty, shoeless children dressed in tattered clothes make the best, most profitable beggars. On street corners they also sell small items, such as real or plastic flowers. Certainly, one of the many reasons Gypsy children do not attend public school regularly is the fact that they are needed during the day to work toward the overall success of the *kumpania*.

The last extra measure of Gypsy middleman economic adaptability is their multioccupational existence. After centuries of economic adaptation to unreliable market situations, Gypsies have learned not to depend upon one source of income. Thus, all Gypsies engage in at least two occupations simultaneously, a practice highly valued among the Gypsies. In fact, the most respected and wealthy Gypsies are those with the greatest spread of occupations. A multioccupational lifestyle adapts to uneven, seasonal, and marginal opportunities. For instance, if the body and fender business is exhausted in a particular territory, all the resources and energies of the group members will shift to roofing, blacktopping driveways, or enhancing a female member's fortunetelling business. The Gypsies' highly fluid labor force is capable of changing businesses in a matter of days.

Strength of Gypsy Culture

The Gypsies provide an interesting case study for the student of middleman minorities. Owing to an uncompromised cultural heritage and highly regulated intraethnic business practices, they endure in the middleman form regardless of changes in the social structure. Although other middleman groups exhibit similar cultural and economic practices, they have, over time, been assimilated to some degree by various dominant societies where they reside (Caudill and De Vos 1956:1102–26; Elazar 1969; Heller 1977:211–47). It is important to ask what makes Gypsies more resistant to assimilation than other middleman minorities.

When I began this research project, I wondered if a society's economic structure could be correlated with the rate at which the Gypsies assimilate within a particular society. My initial hunch was that Gypsies assimilated more readily in societies which demanded it. I thought countries like Sweden and England would be more successful in integrating the Gypsies into their mainstreams because they aggressively implemented social programs with that aim. Likewise, I believed that eastern European communist countries would be even more successful than Sweden and England because of their forceful ideological stance and intolerance of deviant populations within their midst. Finally, I thought a capitalist society like the United States, where Gypsies, enjoying a laissez-faire economy, are more or less invisible to the government would produce the least amount of assimilation. In terms of assimilation into the dominant society, I pondered other variables—intermarriage, observance of the Gypsy religion and customs, participation of Gypsy children in educational institutions, and self-employment. After carefully examining the available evidence, it appears that the Gypsies' rate of assimilation when looking at any of these parameters is negligible. The degree of the pressure or lack of pressure placed upon Gypsies by governments does not affect assimilation rates.

I think Gypsies are able to remain middlemen in any economic or social system despite pressure to assimilate for two reasons: illiteracy and nomadism. Illiteracy prevents the Gypsies from engaging in many types of nonmiddleman economic activity. When a group is illiterate, all medium and high-status jobs are knowingly unattainable to them. On the other hand, they consider manual labor requiring no real literary skills beneath them. Why would they work on a factory assembly line all day for minimum wages with no autonomy when they could be self-employed? Furthermore, literacy opens the door to intellectual, ideological, and cultural activities which have often seduced minority group members into the dominant mainstream. By reducing exposure to new and alien ideas, the Gypsies insulate themselves.

Despite various pressures the Gypsies have also endured as middlemen because they are nomadic. Not being tied to the soil or any geographical location allows them the freedom to move on in the face of adversity. If Gypsy communities were forced to live year after year in one location, they would eventually succumb to some of their hosts' demands. However, because the Gypsy philosophy has always been to move when the *gaje* get too close, their business endeavors have always been as portable as possible.

When one compares the Gypsies with other middlemen, the contrast is sharp. Loewen's (1971) Chinese were geographically tied to the Mississippi Delta by their grocery stores. Jews in eastern Europe were not only tied to businesses but also to synagogues, communal organizations housed in buildings, and ritual baths. The sorrow and reluctance on the part of the Jews to leave Antefkah in the popular musical *Fiddler on the Roof* is based on hundreds of actual accounts (Aleichem 1946, 1949, 1953, 1955; Zborowski and Herzog 1962). The Gypsies do not permit themselves to become attached to any one particular place because history has taught them that sooner or later they will have to move on. As a rule, the Gypsies try to own as few things as possible so they can leave any place at a few hours' notice. When Stalin forced the Gypsies into a collective farm and took their horses away from them, they defiantly burned the farm and its buildings to the ground, made cigarettes out of textbook pages, and fled the scene by train (*Newsweek*, 21 May 1956:55).

An examination of Gypsies as a middleman minority provides illumination on several significant controversies within the field of research. One important controversy is the "sojourner debate." Bonacich (1973:585–90) has argued that it is an unusual attachment to an ancestral homeland that makes middlemen perpetual sojourners. She contends that typically middleman traits like resistance to outmarriage, residential self-segregation, the maintenance of distinctive cultural traits, a tendency to avoid involvement in local politics except in affairs that directly affect their group, and highly organized communities which resist assimilation can be associated with an orientation toward a homeland of origin and a hope of returning there one day (see p. 586).

Other researchers in the field have grappled with this supposed attachment of middlemen to their ancestral homeland. As early as 1952, Siu noted strong ambivalence on the part of Chinese laundrymen in the United States to return to China. Zenner (1976:6–7) has also found problems with the sojourner theory in relationship to the middleman groups he studied.

I believe the Gypsies dispel the notion that a middleman group functions as a nation within a nation owing to an unusual attachment to a homeland. The Gypsies, sojourners for twelve hundred years, have never expressed a desire to return to their land of origin, India. The Gypsy religion, oral tradition, and self-consciousness are devoid of any longing for India. Within their culture, India is no more idealized than any of their former stopping places. In fact, the opposite attitude is common among Gypsies. They do not like being associated with India; they are ashamed of their Indian origins and try to disassociate themselves from India as much as possible. They frequently cite poverty, disease, and the low level of industrial development as reasons for their disassociation.

For the Gypsies, India is history. In this regard they exhibit a strong future-time orientation. They never expect to settle in any one place indefinitely; history has not afforded the Gypsies that luxury. Unlike the Jews, the Gypsies never lamented anything like "next year in Jerusalem." Instead, Gypsies long for a new economic frontier with unlimited potential. The "next year in Jerusalem" dream is substituted by the *Rom*'s "next summer at the terminus of the Alaskan pipeline in Valdez" or "next year in Belize City." Rather than long for the past, the Gypsies aggressively and unsentimentally embrace the future. A quote from an elderly Gypsy makes evident this confident attitude about the future: "You could put me down anywhere in the world and I could earn a living. . . . You could even put me in the desert" (Adams et al. 1975:138).

Bonacich (1973) talks about how host hostility keeps alive love of the homeland, a homeland preserved in the minds of middlemen as "somewhere to go if things get too bad in the host country" (p. 593). But for the Gypsies, this just does not apply. A Romany proverb sums up the lack of connection the Gypsies feel with one special place in the world: Translated, the proverb says: "Anywhere I fall is where I will make my bed." Thus, maintaining a highly organized community and resisting assimilation are not correlated with any intention to return to their land of origin.

Another interesting issue this study raises is whether or not voluntary immigration to a setting is a prerequisite for middleman status. While many of the Gypsies' internal migrations have been voluntary, to seize economic opportunities, some of their movement to settings has been involuntary. Unlike the Jews or the Chinese, the Gypsies were not invited to fill a status gap in a particular society. Usually their arrival was the result of being chased away or expelled from somewhere else. In this respect the Gypsies' middleman skills have been remarkable. It is far easier to fill an available economic niche through invitation than to invent one.

Typically the Gypsies have not been colonized, but they have been used for purposes of colonization, especially in the Americas. Despite the fact that the Gypsies were deported to a setting, they continued to function as middlemen. A striking contrast can be posed between Gypsies and others deported to the New World during colonial times: while other deportees began their stay in the Americas as indentured servants, the Gypsies wandered about independently in self-employed callings.

In conclusion, the Gypsies remain and function as a middleman minority in all societies in which they dwell. The political and social ideologies of any host society have not had significant impact on the Gypsies' cultural or economic way of life. The *Rom* have not assimilated to any observable degree; their fierce retention of the Gypsy way, despite all odds, is a human wonderment and a rare sociological find.

The popular stereotype of the Gypsies as wild, reckless, and lustful wanderers dissolves under sensitive and cautious analysis. The very fact that Gypsies have been overlooked by the discipline of sociology for so long reveals that sociologists, like all others, did not bother to see these people beyond the popular stereotype. If my study accomplishes anything, I hope sociologists and lay people alike will realize the richness, vitality, creativity, and ingenuity of the Gypsy people. During their twelve hundred-year survival in a hostile world, the Gypsies have developed a blueprint for endurance as a middleman minority.

GLOSSARY OF ROMANY WORDS

baro muy	Big mouth
beng	Devil
Biboldo	Jew
bilyah	Handbills; advertising; fortunetelling parlors
bori	Bride or newly married woman
bujo	Literally, a dishcloth; a swindle
ceranda	Quilts
cine ambulante	(Spanish) Traveling cinema companies
dae	Mother
daro	Brideprice
diklo	Scarf to cover the hair of a married Gypsy woman
diwanya	Discussion among male members of the family tribe to settle a dispute
drabarimos	Fortunetelling
familia	Extended family
gaje (plural)	Non-Gypsies
gajo (singular)	Non-Gypsy
glata	children, kids
kris	Gypsy court
kumpania	A group of extended families living, working, and traveling within the same geographic territory
marime	Impure or shameful
masengero	Ritual slaughterer of meat
mulo (singluar)	Ghost of deceased person
mule (plural)	Ghosts of deceased persons
ofisa	Fortunetelling parlor
phuri dae	Old mother; usually the wife of the chief
pohardi	Immodest sitting position for a female Gypsy
pomana	Memorial celebration
posta	Sacrifice
Rom	Refers to the Gypsy people; also the term used for a Gypsy man and husband
Rom baro	"Big man"; chief of a Gypsy *kumpania*
Romania	Traditional Gypsy law
Romany	Name of the Gypsy language
Romen	Soviet Gypsy theater in Moscow

Romni	Married Gypsy woman
sackra	Mother-in-law
tsinivari	Evil spirits that inhabit the night fog
vitsa	A loose federation of extended families who follow the authority of a particular chief
wuzho	Pure; unashamed

NOTES

CHAPTER 1

1. The number is derived from interviews with six Gypsy chiefs in the United States. The same number was given in a recent *Los Angeles Times* article (Dean, 5 October 1986:1).

2. In interviews three Gypsy chiefs in California have told me that by their calculations there are 250,000 Gypsies living in California.

CHAPTER 3

1. Pariah is defined by Webster's *Universal Unabridged Etymological Dictionary* (New York: The World Syndicated Publishing Co., 1936) as "n. tamil paraiyan, drummer, from parai, drum. A pariah was a hereditary drumbeater" (p. 1186).

2. Seljukian was a family which furnished several Turkish dynasties from the eleventh to the thirteenth centuries.

3. The Gypsy word *Rom* has three meanings: (1) *Gypsy*, (2) *man*, and (3) *husband.* See Wedeck 1973:384.

4. The Romany language is also found in the literature as "Romani" and "Romanes."

5. I interviewed Dr. Thaddeus Tate, Director of the Institute of Early American History and Culture at the College of William and Mary on 10 June 1980. I am indebted to him for his help in this aspect of the research.

6. *Virginia Historical Magazine* 2 (1894):100. Professor Tate explained this court ruling: the charge of illegal intercourse, which probably meant that Joane Scot had a baby out of wedlock, only applied to women of the Anglican Church.

7. See Act of Mar. 20, 1930, ch. 131, 1930 Va. Acts of Assembly 346.

8. In 1801, Napoleon Bonaparte recovered the territory of Louisiana which France lost to Spain in 1763.

9. "The Gypsies of Honduras" (*Journal of the Gypsy Lore Society* [ser. 3] 48 [1969]:2–18) chronicles the immigration of Todoro Miklos, known as a Vlaxo (the Walachian), a Kalderash Gypsy who migrated from eastern Europe to South America in 1930 or 1931 and spent a few years in Venezuela and Columbia before ultimately settling in Honduras. He claimed to have cousins in Mexico. Some of my southern California informants are also related to Todoro Miklos. Another extended family I know explained that their grandparents emigrated from eastern Europe to Cuba around 1926.

After living in Havana for a number of years, they emigrated to Mexico City and then finally settled in Los Angeles.

10. This legend was told to Jean-Paul Clébert by José Pirnay, a Gypsy chief in Belgium (see Clébert 1967:26). A similar story was told to me by Dory Costello, a member of a Los Angeles Kalderash tribe.

11. While I was a Visiting Scholar of Holocaust Studies at the University of Nebraska in 1984, Professor Ivan Volgyes in the Department of Political Science informed me that "Biboldo" was a slang term used in pre-World War II Budapest to mean Jew. He said the origin of the word was from the Gypsy quarters of the city. Furthermore, many of my own Gypsy informants have told me that the Romany word for Jew is "Biboldo."

CHAPTER 4

1. The Seven Laws of Noah are: (1) Thou shall believe in God; (2) Thou shall not murder; (3) Thou shall establish a court of justice; (4) Thou shall not eat from an animal while it is alive; (5) Thou shall not be sexually immoral; (6) Thou shall not steal; (7) Thou shall honor thy parents.

2. Lecture given by Rabbi Simcha Wasserman on 29 October 1977, in Los Angeles, entitled "The Seven Laws of Noah."

3. This practice was explained to me by Nick Costello, a Kalderash chief in California, during an interview 20 May 1981.

4. The Gypsies try to give any uneaten food to non-Gypsies. If there are non-Gypsy guests present at the *pomana*, the Gypsies convince them to take the food home with them. This happened to me on 20 May 1981 when I attended the one-year *pomana* of Speedo Montes, a Kalderash Gypsy. Speedo's relatives loaded the entire back seat and trunk of my car with fruit and bread leftover from the *pomana*.

5. Statement by Nick Costello at Speedo Montes's *pomana* on 20 May 1981.

6. For a detailed discussion of the "shoot-out," see David Pickett's article, "Gypsies in Mexico," *Journal of the Gypsy Lore Society* (ser. 3) 44 (1966b):89–90. Also see Frederic Max and Anne Max, "The Gypsies of Honduras," *Journal of the Gypsy Lore Society* (ser. 3) 48 (1969): 2–18. The Max article deals with some of the Gypsies who fled Mexico City after the "shoot-out."

7. Several different informants reported these cases to me. I met the Gypsy who joined the Army at a Fourth of July celebration in 1976. He was living with a non-Gypsy woman because no Gypsies would marry him.

8. Pickett (1966b:92–94) discusses in great detail the lack of faith Mexican Gypsies have in Catholicism. He found them to be "almost totally ignorant of even the most rudimentary and fundamental tenets and dogmas of that faith" (see p. 92).

9. For a detailed discussion of this celebration, see Bart McDowell's *Gypsies, Wanderers of the World* (1970:38–57).

CHAPTER 5

1. When I attended the Toma-Lazlo wedding I heard many of the guests talking about the extremely high bride price.

2. Statement by Frinka Efremo, a Kalderash Gypsy in Los Angeles.

3. Story from Sharon Rainier during an interview, 19 August 1980.

4. David Pickett (1966b:92) has observed that Mexican Gypsies never marry in the Catholic Church.

5. I actually observed this method of gift collecting at the Toma-Lazlo wedding.

CHAPTER 6

1. Based on my fieldwork I have learned that the highest honor bestowed upon a Gypsy is to be asked to serve on a *kris*. Once a Gypsy has proved himself a fair judge, he will be asked by more and more conflicting groups. Usually a chief reaches this high status, and a chief's "court calendar" can become very crowded with *kris* dates. Three of my informants told me that they fly at least twice a month to different cities in the United States to serve on various *krises*.

2. Pickett (1966b:86–87) reports that the Gypsies involved with the traveling cinema operations in Mexico often settle their disputes in *diwanyas* rather than a *kris*. Perhaps this is because they are so geographically isolated from other Gypsies.

3. Information given during an interview with Sharon Rainier, 19 August 1980.

4. The Kuneshti nation has a lower status among Gypsies in the western United States.

5. Reported by a southern California city attorney during a personal interview, July 1976.

6. See Tyrnauer, 1977:43–48.

7. Statement made by a southern California city attorney.

8. This incident was reported by a social worker who specializes in Gypsy cases in northern California.

9. The sign in front of Madame Boswell's Brighton fortunetelling establishment reads: "Member of an ancient Romany family. My grandmother was the palmist to Queen Victoria."

10. Events reported by Bebo and Nancy Stevens, Kalderash Gypsies in Los Angeles. The guilty party was their mother.

11. Fortunetelling is legal in the state of Virginia so long as the practitioner pays the annual $500 license fee. Since the practice is not against the law, all Gypsy fortunetellers advertise in the yellow pages, making my investigation of Gypsy fortunetelling businesses extremely easy there. The law governing fortunetelling is Virginia Tax Code Law s.179a which applies to all persons in the state who are "fortune-tellers, clairvoyants, and practitioners of palmistry and phrenology."

12. Reported in an interview with the landlord, in Ojai, California, 16 March 1981.

13. The following articles appeared in the *Tucson Daily Citizen* and the *Los Angeles Times* on this matter. (Note that the articles, without by-lines, are listed in the references under *Los Angeles Times*.)

Allison Hock, "Weary Gypsy Band Faces Deportation," *Tucson Daily Citizen* (27 February 1974):1–2.

Dave Smith, "Left in Arizona Desert: One Hundred Gypsies From Europe Smuggled Into U.S., Robbed," *Los Angeles Times* (27 February 1974):3,17.

"Ace in the Hole on Deportation, Gypsy Families Enjoy 'Last Laugh' at U.S." *Los Angeles Times* (5 March 1974a):17.

"Gypsy Band: Where Do Yugo From Here?" (24 April 1974b):38.

"Diplomatic Snafu, Deported Gypsies Camping in Chicago," *Los Angeles Times* (9 July 1947c):19.

CHAPTER 7

1. *Bujo*, directly translated from Romany, means dishcloth. It has become a slang word among the Gypsies to describe a certain type of swindle. During a fortunetelling interaction, a gullible client is told that his or her money is cursed; if the client is willing to place the money in a special cloth (usually a washcloth), it will be blessed and all of the client's troubles will disappear. The *bujo* with the money is exchanged for a *bujo* filled with paper. The client is told not to open the cloth for three days. By the time the client realizes he or she has been cheated, the Gypsies have left town.

2. This activity was confirmed by statements of two sociologists at George Madison University at Harrisburg, Virginia: Bruce Busching, Ph.D., and Mary Lou Wiley, Ph.D.

3. In an interview with the Johnsons, Kalderash Gypsies living and working in Williamsburg, they mentioned that they travel to Chase City every summer to work at the county fair. The city attorney's remark corroborated their story.

4. Members of the traveling cinema regularly buy large tarpaulins from my father.

5. Information about welfare was provided to me by a "Gypsies' social worker" in central California, 19 August 1980. This monthly breakdown was regarded by the social worker as "typical" for a Gypsy family in her district.

CHAPTER 8

1. I have heard this story independently from three Gypsy chiefs, one of whom originally called the *kris* to find a location for these Gypsies. This

chief, the most powerful Machwaya chief in the United States, took a special interest in the Yugoslav Gypsies because they were also Machwaya.

2. I observed Gypsies working in all of these capacities when I was in Yugoslavia in 1974.

3. Several Soviet Jewish emigrés in Los Angeles told me that the most popular folk singer in the Soviet Union is a Gypsy man known as Slichenko; his most famous song is "Black Eyes."

4. Information obtained from Isaac Byk in the clothing salvage business in Stockholm; many of his suppliers are Gypsies.

REFERENCES

Acton, Thomas.
1972   World Romani Congress. *Journal of the Gypsy Lore Society* (ser. 3) 51:96–101.
1974   *Gypsy Politics and Social Change.* London: Routledge and Kegan Paul.
Adams, Barbara, Judith Okely, David Morgan, and David Smith.
1975   *Gypsies and Government Policy in England.* London: Heinemann.
Aleichem, Sholom.
1946   *The Old Country.* Translated by Julius and Frances Butwin. New York: Crown Publishers.
1949   *Tevyeh's Daughters.* Translated by Frances Butwin. New York: Crown Publishers.
1953   *Adventures of Mottel, the Cantor's Son.* Translated by Tamara Kahana. New York: Abelord-Schuman.
1955   *The Great Fair.* Translated by Tamara Kahana. New York: Noonday Press.
Allport, Gordon.
1958   *The Nature of Prejudice.* New York: Doubleday Anchor Books.
Andree, Richard.
1911–12 Old Warning-Placards for Gypsies. *Journal of the Gypsy Lore Society* (ser. 2)5:202–4.
Andreski, Stanislav.
1963   An Economic Interpretation of Anti-Semitism in Eastern Europe. *Jewish Journal of Sociology* 5:201–13.
Baltzar, Sven.
1973   *The Gypsies in Sweden.* IMFO-Group. Institute of Education, University of Stockholm.
Bartels, E. D., and G. Brun.
1943   *Gypsies in Denmark—A Social-Biological Study.* Copenhagen.
Barth, Fredrik.
1955   The Social Organization of a Pariah Group in Norway. *Norveg* (Oslo) 5:125–44.
1969   *Ethnic Groups and Boundaries.* Boston: Little Brown & Co.
Bataillard, Paul
1889   Beginning of the Immigration of The Gypsies into Western Europe in the Fifteenth Century. *Journal of the Gypsy Lore Society* (ser. 1) 4:185–212.

Bercovici, Konrad.
1929   *The Story of the Gypsies*. London.
Beier, A. L.
1974   Vagrants and The Social Order in Elizabethan England. *Past and Present* 64:3–29.
Beynon, Erdmann Doane.
1936   The Gypsy in a Non-Gypsy Economy. *American Journal of Sociology* 42:358–70.
Blalock, Hubert M.
1967   *Toward a Theory of Minority-Group Relations*. New York: Capricorn Books.
Block, Martin.
1939   *Gypsies: Their Life and Their Customs*. Translated by Barbara Kucznynski and Duncan Taylor. New York: Appleton-Century.
Boles, Jacqueline, and Don Boles.
1959   The Gypsies' Doctor in Georgia. *Journal of the Gypsy Lore Society* (ser. 3) 38:55–63.
Bonacich, Edna.
1972   A Theory of Ethnic Antagonism: The Split Labor Market. *American Sociological Review* 37:547–59.
1973   A Theory of Middleman Minorities. *American Sociological Review* 38:583–94.
1974   Reply to Stryker. *American Sociological Review* 39:282.
Bonacich, Edna, and John Modell.
1980   *The Economic Basis of Ethnic Solidarity: A Study of Japanese-Americans*. Berkeley: University of California Press.
Bronsztejn, S.
1963   The Jewish Population of Poland in 1931. *Jewish Journal of Sociology* 5:3–29.
Brown, Irving.
1922   *Nights and Days on the Gypsy Trail*. New York: Harper & Bros.
1924   *Gypsy Fires in America*. New York: Harper & Bros.
1928   Roms are Doms. *Journal of the Gypsy Lore Society* (ser. 3) 7:170–77.
1929   The Gypsies in America. *Journal of the Gypsy Lore Society* (ser. 3) 8:145–75.
Cahnman, Werner J.
1974   Pariahs, Strangers, and Court Jews: A Conceptual Clarification. *Sociological Analysis* 35:155–66.
Caudill, William, and George De Vos.
1956   Achievement, Culture and Personality: The Case of the Japanese Americans. *American Anthropologist* 58:1102–26.
Christian Century.
1971   European Gypsy Leaders Ask For Recognition. (ser. 5) 28:519.

Civic Trust.
1967–68 *Disposal of Unwanted Vehicles and Bulky Refuse.* London: Graphic Press, Ltd.
Clébert, Jean Paul.
1967 *The Gypsies.* Translated by Charles Duff. Harmondsworth: Penguin Books.
Coelho, F.
1892 *The Gypsies of Portugal.* Lisbon: Imprensa Nacional.
Cohn, Werner.
1969 Some Comparisons Between Gypsy (North American rom) and American English Kinship Terms. *American Anthropologist* (71):476–82.
1973 *The Gypsies.* Reading, Mass.: Addison-Wesley.
Cotten, Rena.
1951 Sex Dichotomy Among the American Kalderash Gypsies. *Journal of the Gypsy Lore Society* (ser. 3) 30:16–25.
Dean, Paul.
1986 Gypsies Are Banding Together to Fight Age-old Stereotypes. *Los Angeles Times* 5 October 1986:1,10,11.
Dodds, Norman.
1966 *Gypsies, Didikois, and Other Travellers.* London: Johnson Publications.
Dostal, Walter.
1957 Personality and Culture Conflict of the Austrian Gypsies. *Journal of the Gypsy Lore Society* (ser. 3) 36.
Eisenberg, Howard.
1979 Those Splendid Syrians: Weekend in Deal. *Jewish Living,* September-October:37–40.
Eitzen, D. Stanley.
1972 Two Minorities: the Jews of Poland and the Chinese of the Philippines. Reprinted in *Majority and Minority: the Dynamics of Racial and Ethnic Relations,* edited by Norman Yetman and C. Hoy Steele, 117–38. Boston: Allyn & Bacon.
Elazar, Daniel J.
1969 American Political Theory and the Political Notions of American Jews: Convergences and Contradictions. In *The Ghetto and Beyond,* edited by Peter I. Rose, 203–27. New York: Random House.
Fisher, Marna F.
1965 Gypsies. In *Minority Problems,* edited by Caroline B. Rose and Arnold M. Rose, 50–54. New York: Harper & Row.
Foletier, Francois De Vaux.
1961 *Les Tsiganes dans l'ancienne France.* Paris: Connaissance du Monde.

1962   Gypsy Captains in Provence and the Rhone Valley in the 16th and 17th centuries. *Journal of the Gypsy Lore Society* (ser. 3) 41:3–10.

1968   La Grande Rafle des Bohemiens du Pays Basque Sous Le Consulat. *Études de Tsiganes* (March):13–22.

Fontane, Theodore.

1892   *Effi Briest.* Translated by Douglas Parmée. Reprint. Baltimore: Penguin Books, 1967.

1896   *Frau Tres Belle.* Translated by Gabriele Annan. Reprint. Chicago: University of Chicago Press, 1979.

Freedman, Maurice.

1959   Jews, Chinese, and Some Others. *The British Journal of Sociology* 10:61–70.

Gaster, M.

1923   Bill of Sale of Gypsy slaves in Moldavia, 1851. *Journal of the Gypsy Lore Society* (ser. 3) 2:68–81.

Gilliat-Smith, Bernard.

1948   The Gypsies in Bulgaria (1948). *Journal of the Gypsy Lore Society* (ser. 3) 27:156–57.

Godden, Rumer.

1973   *The Diddakoi.* Boston: G. K. Hall.

Goulet, Denis and Marco Walshok.

1971   Values Among Underdevelopment Marginals: The Case of Spanish Gypsies. *Comparative Studies in Society and History* 13:451–72.

Grellman, H. M. G.

1787   *Historischer Versuch über die Zigeuner.* English edition. Gottingen: Dieterich, 1807.

Gropper, Rena Cotten.

1975   *Gypsies in the City.* Princeton, N.J.: The Darwin Press.

Gustafsson, Inga.

1973   *Studies of a Minority Group's Efforts to Preserve Its Cultural Autonomy.* IMFO-GROUP, Institute of Education, University of Stockholm.

Guy, Willy.

1975a   Ways of Looking at Roms: The Case of Czechoslovakia. In *Gypsies, Tinkers and Other Travellers,* edited by Farnham Rehfisch, 201–30. London: Academic Press.

1975b   Foreword to *Gypsies in Czechoslovakia,* by Josef Koudelka. New York: Aperture.

Haley, William John.

1934   The Gypsy Conference at Bucharest. *Journal of the Gypsy Lore Society* (ser. 3) 13:182–90.

Hall, Elsie M.

1932   Gentile Cruelty to Gypsies. *Journal of the Gypsy Lore Society* (ser. 3) 11:49–56.

Halliday, W. R.
1922   Some Notes Upon the Gypsies of Turkey. *Journal of the Gypsy Lore Society* (ser. 3) 1:163–89.
Hancock, Ian.
1980   Gypsies. In Harvard *Encyclopedia of American Ethnic Groups*, edited by Stephan Thernstrom, 440–45. Cambridge: Harvard University Press.
Hannan, Michael.
1979   The Dynamics of Ethnic Boundaries in Modern States. In *National Development and the World System: Educational, Economical, and Political Change, 1900–1970*, edited by John Mayer and Michael Hannan, 253–75. Chicago: University of Chicago Press.
Harvey, Denis, and C. H. Ward Jackson.
1973   *The English Gypsy Caravan.* New York: Drake Publishers, Inc.
Heller, Celia S.
1977   *On the Edge of Destruction: Jews of Poland Between the Two World Wars.* New York: Columbia University Press.
Herford, R. Travers
1969   *Pirke Aboth. The Ethics of the Talmud Sayings of the Fathers.* New York: Schocken Books.
Hock, Allison.
1974   "Weary Gypsy Band Faces Deportation," *Tucson Daily Citizen* 27 February:1–2.
Horváth, Mihály.
1971   Demographic Data of Gypsy Women Giving Birth to a Child in the Siklos District in 1961–1971. Demográfia 14:366–71.
Katz, Jacob.
1961   *Exclusiveness and Tolerance: Jewish-Gentile Relations in Medieval and Modern Times.* New York: Schocken Books.
Kenrick, Donald and Grattan Puxon.
1972   *The Destiny of Europe's Gypsies.* New York: Basic Books.
Kephart, William M.
1982   *Extraordinary Groups: The Sociology of Unconventional Life-Styles.* 2d ed. New York: St. Martin's Press.
Kitov, A. E.
1974   *The Jew and His Home.* New York: Shengold Publishers.
Kolatch, Alfred J.
1981   *The Jewish Book of Why.* Middle Village, New York: Jonathan David Publishers, Inc.
Koudelka, Josef.
1975   *Gypsies in Czechoslovakia.* New York: Aperture.
Lauwagie, Beverly Nagel.
1979   Ethnic Boundaries in Modern States: Romano Lavo-Lil Revisited. *American Journal of Sociology* 85:310–36.

Lee, Ronald.
   1972   Goddam Gypsy. Indianapolis, Ind.: Bobbs-Merrill.
Leland, Charles G.
   1894   The English Gypsies and Their Language. London: Trubner &
           Co.
   1886   The Gypsies. Boston: Houghton Mifflin Co.
Levin, Nora.
   1973   The Holocaust. New York: Schocken Books.
Levinson, Robert E.
   1978   The Jews in the California Gold Rush. New York: KTAV Pub-
           lishing House, Inc.
Levy, Juliette de Bairacli.
   1962   A Gypsy in New York. London: Faber & Faber.
Light, Ivan H.
   1972   Ethnic Enterprise in America: Business and Welfare Among
           Chinese, Japanese, and Blacks. Berkeley: University of Califor-
           nia Press.
   1977   The Ethnic Vice District, 1890–1944. American Sociological
           Review 42:464–79.
   1979   Disadvantaged Minorities in Self-Employment. International
           Journal of Comparative Sociology 20:31–45.
Lloyd, Theodosia.
   1965   Gypsies in Bruges and Avignon. Journal of the Gypsy Lore So-
           ciety (ser. 3) 44:155–56.
Loewen, James W.
   1971   The Mississippi Chinese: Between Black and White. Cam-
           bridge, Mass.: Harvard University Press.
Loewenberg, Peter.
   1977   Lecture. University of California, Los Angeles, 25 January.
Lopez, Andre, and Jan Yoors.
   1974   The Gypsies of Spain. New York: Macmillan Co.
Los Angeles Times.
   1974a   March 5. "Ace In The Hole On Deportation: Gypsy Families
           Enjoy Last Laugh at U.S.," 17.
   1974b   April 24. "Postscript: Gypsy band: Where Do Yugo From
           Here?" 38.
   1974c   July 9. "Diplomatic Snafu, Deported Gypsies Camping in Chi-
           cago," 19.
Maas, Peter.
   1975   King of the Gypsies. New York: Viking Press.
Macfie, R. A. Scott.
   1943   Gypsy Persecutions: A Survey of a Black Chapter in European
           History. Journal of the Gypsy Lore Society (ser. 3) 22:65–78.

MacLeod, George.
1909   A New World Gypsy Camp. *Journal of the Gypsy Lore Society* (ser. 2) 3:81–88.

Malnick, Bertha.
1959   The Moscow Gypsy Theatre, 1957–8. *Journal of the Gypsy Lore Society* (ser. 3) 38:81–85.

Mano, K.
1973   Gimlet Eye: Future of Fortune-Tellers. *National Review*, 25, 23 (8 June):636.

Max, Frederic, and Anne Max.
1969   The Gypsies of Honduras. *Journal of the Gypsy Lore Society* (ser. 3) 48:2–18.

Maximoff, Matéo.
1946   Germany and the Gypsies. *Journal of the Gypsy Lore Society* (ser. 3) 25:104–8.
1949   *The Ursitory.* London: Chapman & Hall.
1965   The Evangelical Gypsies in France. *Journal of the Gypsy Lore Society* (ser. 3) 44:151–53.

McDowell, Bart.
1970   *Gypsies: Wanderers of the World.* Rockville: National Geographic Society, Fawcett Printing Corp.

McLaughlin, John B.
1980   *Gypsy Lifestyles.* Lexington, Mass.: Lexington Books.

Miller, Carol J.
1975   Machwaya Gypsy Marime. In *Gypsies, Tinkers and Other Travellers*, edited by Farnham Rehfisch, 41–54. London: Academic Press.

Mitchell, J.
1942   King of the Gypsies. *New Yorker* 18 (15 August):21–35.
1955   "Profiles—The Beauty Flower." *New Yorker* 31 (4 June):39–89.

Meiselman, Moshe.
1978   *Jewish Woman in Jewish Law.* New York: KTAV Publishing House, Inc.

Mulcohy, F. D.
1976   Gitano Sex Role Symbolism and Behavior. *Anthropological Quarterly* 49:135–51.

Murin, S.
1949   Hawaii's Gypsies. *Social Process in Hawaii* 14:14–37.

Newsweek.
1956   "Bigger than Brinks." (21 May):55.

Okely, Judith.
1975   Gypsies Travelling in Southern England. In *Gypsies, Tinkers and Other Travellers*, edited by Farnham Rehfisch, 55–84. London: Academic Press.
1983   *The Traveller—Gypsies.* Cambridge: Cambridge University Press.

Oujevolk, George B.
1935   The Gypsies of Brooklyn in 1934. *Journal of the Gypsy Lore Society* (ser. 3) 14:121–27.
Pankok, Otto.
1953   The Gypsies in Germany Today. *Journal of the Gypsy Lore Society* (ser. 3) 32:152–54.
Pickett, David W.
1965   The Gypsies in Mexico. *Journal of the Gypsy Lore Society* (ser. 3) 44:81–99.
1966a   The Gypsies in Mexico. *Journal of the Gypsy Lore Society* (ser. 3) 45:6–17.
1966b   The Gypsies in Mexico. *Journal of the Gypsy Lore Society* (ser. 3) 45:84–99.
Puxon, Grattan.
1968   *On the Road, Report of Gypsies and Civil Liberties.* London: The National Council for Civil Liberties.
1969   Gypsies and the Czech Crisis. *Journal of the Gypsy Lore Society* (ser. 3) 48:57–59.
1976   Gypsies: Blacks of East Europe. *Nation* 222, 15:460–64.
Quintana, Bertha B. and Lois Floyd.
1972   *Que Gitano! Gypsies of Southern Spain.* New York: Holt, Rinehart & Winston, Inc.
Rao, Aparna.
1975   Some Manus Conceptions and Attitudes. In *Gypsies, Tinkers and Other Travellers*, edited by Farnham Rehfisch, 139–68. London: Academic Press.
Rakoczi, Basil Ivan.
1961   An Artist's Visit to the Gypsies of Southern France and the U.S.S.R. *Journal of the Gypsy Lore Society* (ser. 3) 40:120–27.
Rehfisch, Farnham.
1975   *Gypsies, Tinkers, and Other Travellers.* London: Academic Press.
Rinder, Irwin.
1958   Strangers in The Land. *Social Problems* 6:253–60.
Roberts, Samuel.
1830   *Parallel Miracles; Or, The Jews and the Gypsies.* London: Blackwell Printers.
1836   *The Gypsies: Their Origin, Continuance, and Destination.* London: Longman Co.
Rosenfield, Paul.
1978   It's Just The Gypsy in His Script. *Los Angeles Times* 22 February:26–27.
Rosenthal, A. M.
1959   Gypsies Fiddle While Warsaw Burns. *New York Times Magazine* (12 April):31–32.
Rudiger, K.
1938   Parasiten der Gemeinschaft. *Volk u Rasse*, pp. 87–89.

Salo, Matt, and Shelia Salo.
1977   *The Kalderash in Eastern Canada.* Ottawa: National Museums of Canada.
Sampson, John.
1923   On the Origins and Early Migrations of the Gypsies. *Journal of the Gypsy Lore Society* (ser. 3) 2:156–69.
San Roman, Teresa.
1975   Kinship, Marriage, Law and Leadership in Two Urban Gypsy Settlements in Spain. In *Gypsies, Tinkers and Other Travellers,* edited by Farnham Rehfisch, 169–200. London: Academic Press.
Schechtman, Joseph B.
1966   The Gypsy Problem. *Midstream Magazine* 12 (November):52–60.
Schermerhorn, R. A.
1970   *Comparative Ethnic Relations.* New York: Random House.
Seago, Edward.
1937   *Caravan.* London: Collins.
Sergievskij, M. V.
1933   Book Review of Gypsies of the Ukraine. *Journal of the Gypsy Lore Society* (ser. 3) 12:52–54.
Shibutani, T. and K. Kwan.
1965   *Ethnic Stratification.* New York: Macmillan.
Simmel, Georg.
1906   The Sociology of Secrecy and of Secret Societies. Translated by Albion Small. *American Journal of Sociology* 11:441–98.
1950   *The Sociology of Georg Simmel.* Edited and translated by Kurt H. Wolff. New York: The Free Press.
1966   *Conflict and the Web of Group Affiliation.* Translated by Kurt H. Wolff. New York: The Free Press.
Siu, Paul C. P.
1952   The Sojourner. *American Journal of Sociology* 58:34–44.
Smith, Dave.
1974   "Left in Arizona Desert: One Hundred Gypsies From Europe Smuggled into U.S., Robbed." *Los Angeles Times* (27 February):1,18.
Soller, Ignacy.
1938   Coronation of a Polish Gypsy King. *Journal of the Gypsy Lore Society* (ser. 3) 17:71–73.
Sombart, Werner.
1951   *The Jews and Modern Capitalism.* Translated by M. Epstein. New York: Collier Books.
Stanford, Jeremy.
1973   *Gypsies.* London: Secker & Warburg.
Starkie, Walter.
1937   *Don Gypsy.* New York: E. P. Dutton & Co., Inc.
1953   *In Sara's Tent.* London: John Murray, Ltd.

Stonequist, Everett.
1961   *The Marginal Man.* New York: Russell & Russell.
Stryker, Sheldon.
1974   A Theory of Middleman Minorities: A Comment. *American Sociological Review* 39:281.
Sutherland, Anne.
1975a   Gypsies: The Hidden Americans. *Society* 12:27–33.
1975b   *Gypsies: The Hidden Americans.* New York: Free Press.
Sway, Marlene.
1975   Gypsies as a Perpetual Minority: A Case Study. *Humboldt Journal of Social Relations* 3 (Fall–Winter):48–55.
1977   The Role of the American Gypsy Woman. Paper presented at Annual Meeting of the Western Social Science Association, Denver, Colorado.
1980a   Gypsies and Their Health Care in the United States: The Special Case of the Gypsy Woman. Paper presented at the Annual Meeting of the Western Social Science Association, Albuquerque, New Mexico.
1980b   Gypsies and Their Use of Non-Gypsy Health Care Services in the United States. Paper presented at the Alpha Kappa Delta Sociological Research Symposium, Richmond, Va.
1981   Simmel's Concept of the Stranger and the Gypsies. *The Social Science Journal* 18:41–50.
Taikon, Katarina:
1967   *Zigenare Ar Vi.* Stockholm: Norstedts.
1970   *Forlat Att Vi Stor.* Stockholm: Norstedts.
Takman, John.
1976   *The Gypsies in Sweden: A Socio-Medical Study.* Stockholm: Liber Forlag.
Taylor, Philip.
1971   *The Distant Magnet: European Emigration to the U.S.A.* New York: Harper Touchstone Books.
Thompson, T. W.
1922   The Uncleanness of Women among English Gypsies. *Journal of the Gypsy Lore Society* (ser. 3) 1:15–43.
Tillhagen, Carl-Herman.
1947   A Swedish Gypsy Investigation. *Journal of the Gypsy Lore Society* (ser.3) 26:89–115.
1949   Gypsy Clans in Sweden. *Journal of the Gypsy Lore Society* (ser. 3) 28:1–17.
1950   Gypsy Clans in Sweden. *Journal of the Gypsy Lore Society* (ser. 3) 29:23–39.
1952   Funeral and Death Customs of the Swedish Gypsies. *Journal of the Gypsy Lore Society* (ser. 3) 31:29–54.
1953a   Betrothal and Wedding Customs Among the Swedish Gypsies. *Journal of the Gypsy Lore Society* (ser. 3) 32:13–30.

1953b   Betrothal and Wedding Customs Among the Swedish Gypsies. *Journal of the Gypsy Lore Society* (sec. 3) 32:106–24.

1955   Married Life and Family Life Among the Swedish Kalderasa Gypsies. *Journal of the Gypsy Lore Society* (ser. 3) 34:2–29.

1956   Diseases and Their Cure Among the Swedish Gypsies. *Journal of the Gypsy Lore Society* (ser. 3) 35:49–62.

1957a   Food and Drink Among The Swedish Kalderasa Gypsies. *Journal of the Gypsy Lore Society* (ser. 3) 36:25–52.

1957b   The Gypsy Problem In Sweden. *Journal of the Gypsy Lore Society* (ser. 3) 36:88–104.

1958a   The Gypsy Problem in Finland. *Journal of the Gypsy Lore Society* (ser. 3) 37:41–50.

1958b   Conception of Justice Among the Swedish Gypsies. *Journal of the Gypsy Lore Society* (ser. 3) 37:82–96.

1959a   Conception of Justice among the Swedish Gypsies. *Journal of the Gypsy Lore Society* (ser. 3) 38:18–31.

1959b   Conception of Justice among the Swedish Gypsies. *Journal of the Gypsy Lore Society* (ser 3) 38:127–34.

1967   Welfare Benefits from the Government for the Gypsies in Sweden. *Journal of the Gypsy Lore Society* (ser. 3) 46:23–34.

Tipler, Derek.
1968   From Nomads to Nation. *Midstream Magazine* 14 (7 July):61–70.

1969   The Colteshti. *Journal of the Gypsy Lore Society* (ser. 3) 48:27–33.

Tompkins, Janet.
1965   Gypsies in Richmond. Report to Welfare Department, Richmond, Calif. Part III, 1–16.

1971   Gypsy Attitudes towards Medical Care: Theories of Disease, Magic, Healing, and Cure. Unpublished lecture to the Children's Hospital, San Francisco, Calif.

Torgerson, Dial.
1980   Jerusalem's Gypsies Remain Pariahs. *Los Angeles Times*, 7 August: 14–15.

Trankell, Arne, and Ingrid Trankell.
1968   Problems of the Swedish Gypsies. *Scandinavian Journal for Educational Research* (22):141–214.

Trigg, Elwood B.
1968   Religion and Social Reform among the Gypsies of Britain. *Journal of the Gypsy Lore Society* (ser. 3) 47:82–109.

1973   *Gypsies, Demons, and Divinities.* Secaucus, N.J.: Citadel Press.

Tyrnauer, Gabrielle.
1977   *Gypsies in the State of Washington: A Report to the Bicentennial Commission.* Olympia, Washington: State Printing Office.

Ulć, Otto.
1972   Communist National Minority Policy: the Case of the Gypsies in Czechoslovakia. Reprinted in *Majority and Minority: the Dynamics of Racial and Ethnic Relations,* edited by Norman Yetman and C. Hoy Steele, 138–46. Boston: Allyn & Bacon.

Van Kappen, O.
1962   Three Dutch Safe Conducts for Heidens. *Journal of the Gypsy Lore Society* (ser. 3) 41:89–100.
1965   A Contribution to the History of the Gypsies in the Bishopric of Liege, 1540–1726. *Journal of the Gypsy Lore Society* (ser. 3) 44:49–56.
1969   A Contribution to the History of the Gypsies in Belgium. *Journal of the Gypsy Lore Society* (ser. 3) 48:107–120.

Vesey-FitzGerald, Brian.
1944   Gypsy Medicine. *Journal of the Gypsy Lore Society* (ser. 3) 23:21–50.
1973   *Gypsies of Britain.* Newton Abbot: David & Charles.

Vukanović, T. P.
1961   The Manufacture of Pots and Pans Among the Gypsies of Kosovo and Metohija. *Journal of the Gypsy Lore Society* (ser. 3) 40:35–44.

Wade, R. A. R.
1968   A Conference of Public Health Inspection on Gypsies. *Journal of the Gypsy Lore Society* (ser. 3) 47:116–33.

Weber, Max.
1952   *Ancient Judaism.* Translated and edited by Hans H. Gerth and Don Martindale. Glencoe, Ill.: The Free Press.
1968   *Economy and Society.* 3 vols. Edited by Guenther Roth and Hans Wittich. New York: Bedminster Press.

Wedeck, H. E.
1973   *Dictionary of Gypsy Life and Lore.* London: Peter Owen.

Weybright, Victor.
1938   Who Can Tell the Gypsies' Fortune? The Nomad Coppersmith, Now at the End of the Gypsy Trail. *Survey Graphic* 27 (March):142–45.
1945   A Nomad Gypsy Coppersmith in New York. *Journal of the Gypsy Lore Society* (ser. 3) 24:2–8.

Wiesenthal, Simon.
1967   *The Murderers Among Us.* New York: McGraw-Hill.

Winstedt, E. O.
1932   Some Records of the Gypsies in Germany, 1407–1792. *Journal of the Gypsy Lore Society* (ser. 3) 11:123–41.

Wirth, Louis.
1928   *The Ghetto.* Chicago: University of Chicago Press.

Wirtz, E.
1954   Gypsies in Bavaria. *Journal of the Gypsy Lore Society* (ser. 3) 33:165–68.

Wood, M. F.
  1973　　*In the Life of a Romany Gypsy.* London: Routledge & Kegan
　　　　　Paul.
Yates, Dora.
  1949　　Hitler and the Gypsies. *Commentary* 8 (November):455–59.
  1953　　*My Gypsy Days: Recollections of a Romani Rawnie.* London:
　　　　　Phoenix House, Ltd.
Yoors, Jan.
  1947　　Lowari Law and Jurisdiction. *Journal of the Gypsy Lore Society*
　　　　　(ser. 3) 26:1–18.
  1967　　*The Gypsies.* New York: A Touchstone Book, Simon &
　　　　　Schuster.
  1971　　*Crossing: A Journal of Survival and Resistance in World War
　　　　　II.* London: Weidenfeld & Nicolson.
Zborowski, Mark, and Elizabeth Herzog.
  1962　　*Life Is With People.* New York: Schocken.
Zenner, Walter P.
  1976　　Middleman Minority Theories: A Critical Review. Paper pre-
　　　　　sented at the Conference on the New Immigration, Smithso-
　　　　　nian Institution, Washington, D.C.

INDEX

A Note on the Author

Marlene Sway received her B.A., M.A., and Ph.D. in sociology from the University of California, Los Angeles. She was a Visiting Fellow at the University of Miami and served as Distinguished Visiting Scholar of Holocaust Studies at the University of Nebraska, Lincoln and Omaha. Dr. Sway was also a Distinguished Lecturer of the Holocaust at the Maurice Greenberg Center for Judaic Studies at the University of Hartford, Hartford, Connecticut. She has taught sociology at the University of Utah and the University of Alabama at Tuscaloosa. Currently she is a Research Associate in the Department of Sociology at the University of Alabama—Birmingham. Ms. Sway has published articles on Gypsies, minority business, and the Holocaust in *Urban Life*, the *Social Science Journal*, and the *Journal of Sociology and Social Welfare*.